JUMPING mouse
a story about inner trust

JUMPING mouse

a story about inner trust

Mary Elizabeth Marlow

HAMPTON ROADS
PUBLISHING COMPANY, INC.

For information write:

Hampton Roads Publishing Company, Inc.
134 Burgess Lane
Charlottesville, VA 22902

Or call: (804) 296-2772
FAX: (804) 296-5096
e-mail: hrpc@mail.hamptonroadspub.com
Internet: http://www.hamptonroadspub.com

If you are unable to order this book from your local
bookseller, you may order directly from the publisher.
Quantity discounts for organizations are available.
Call 1-800-766-8009, toll-free.

ISBN 1-57174-014-7

11 10 9 8 7 6 5 4 3 2

Printed on acid-free paper in Canada

Dedication

To Ann Maria,
My Dear Friend,

Whose Heart is Open
Who Walks in Total Trust
Who Sees with the Eyes of an Eagle

Contents

Preface

An East Indian teacher once challenged a group of students to share *one truth* that they knew. Immediately, hands went up. Each person, in turn, confidently shared impressive bits of knowledge and information, for these were students with academic accolades and advanced studies in metaphysics. The teacher listened patiently as each person took his turn, then spoke with a piercing clarity. "What you have shared is not what you know. It is only what you have learned from someone else. It is borrowed truth. Go off by yourselves. Take as long as you need. Re-examine your lives, your experiences. Come back only when you have discovered something you personally know."

What this teacher knew, and perhaps what we all sense at some inextricable level, is that to know and to trust our own truth is probably the single most challenging issue any of us ever face. We long to have the courage to trust within.

On a personal level, men and women alike are confronted with the dilemma of not knowing how to trust. As a society, we are sobered by the reality that much of what we have trusted in our political, religious, economic, and social world is in flux. If, as a people, our trust is solely in external form, we are in jeopardy. If, on the other hand, we know and trust our own inner truth, it is easier to sense what is trustworthy in our outer world. We are less likely to be misled, or thrown off balance, or pulled in conflicting directions. Both personally and collectively, we need to re-examine who and what we trust. We want to know when to, whether to, and how to trust.

Some years ago, I heard a story that spoke about trust in a voice all its own. The story, *Jumping Mouse*, is an ancient legend from the Native American tradition. I felt as though I had been waiting for this story my entire life; it touched my soul with a resounding chord of resonance. I wept from a deep place within. I knew it was my story, for the issue of trust has been a major theme in my personal mythology. And I knew it was not just my story; at some level it is everyone's story.

Jumping Mouse is ancient in origin but timely in concept. It is a compelling story of initiation told in the language of the heart. It is whimsical, yet profound. In this legend, a mouse leaves the familiar, undertakes heroic tasks, meets overwhelming obstacles, makes difficult choices, and resolves paradoxes. As Jumping Mouse faces the mosaic of challenges demanding more and more courage to trust within, we journey alongside him and interface with our own obstacles. We face confusion, doubt, and fear and reawaken innocence and trust in the moment and in ourselves. In the end, we are empowered, for *Jumping Mouse* is a triumph of the Soul.

Perhaps your experience with this story will be similar to mine. Once heard, this story becomes an integral part of the listener. It never leaves. It continually calls us to remember who we are. With each telling, there are new discoveries, and the heart is opened a bit more. It may be that the full disclosure of its deeper mysteries is a lifetime task.

I tell the story as it speaks to me, and continues to speak—with a plethora of feelings, memories, images, and metaphors, and with other stories which juxtapose themselves alongside *Jumping Mouse*.

As you read, I invite you to pause along the way. Sense your own inner alliance with the collective wisdom of the story. Allow your spirit to take flight and soar far beyond the pages of this book to the heart of your own truth.

Acknowledgements

I wish to acknowledge the following people for their invaluable contributions to this book:

The Plains Indian People of the Native American tradition for their gift of this sacred story;

Corrine, a beautiful Seneca Indian woman, who came to be a part of our family when I was born, who nurtured and cared for me, and imparted in me a love for the Native American people, their songs, and their stories;

Joseph Rael (Beautiful Painted Arrow), without whom I may have wandered the world over without ever being introduced to the wisdom of the Ancient Ones;

The late Paul Solomon, who awakened in me a love for the unifying Spirit in all traditions;

John Nelson, author and long-time friend, invaluable sounding board and critic throughout the writing of this book, who insisted on more when I would have settled for less;

Kathy Grotz and Jean Reeder for painstaking and careful editing and proofing;

Lynne Paine, dear friend and fellow therapist, for encouragement and empowerment;

My many friends throughout the world, representing diverse traditions from many different countries, who have honored me with their sacred stories and in so doing have demonstrated that amid diversity there is the One Great Spirit.

CHAPTER ONE
Mouse Village

Life In Mouse Village

Once there was a mouse named Jeremy who, like all the other mice, lived in a little village hidden away in the woods. He was always busy, running and jumping, hurrying and scurrying to and fro. It seemed he was always in motion. In fact, he hardly ever stood still. And, like the other mice, he couldn't see very far. Nor was he able to see very clearly. For mice, as you may have noticed, usually have their whiskers in the ground.

Several years ago, I was asked to conduct a day-long counseling session with a "very busy" family of seven. This was a particularly prestigious family. Every member of the family was academically distinguished and highly accomplished. As they entered the therapy room, my first impression was that they were one of the "busiest" families I had ever seen. They quickly began rearranging furniture, fluffing pillows, talking non-stop all the while. Eventually, we sat down and began our day together. It became obvious that the busyness was more than a momentary attempt to camouflage their nervousness about the upcoming session. It was a coping mechanism to which they were accustomed, one they used frequently to avoid having to relate at deeper levels. The family had been so frenzied over the years that they had often overlooked some important needs. For mice are always busy, hurrying and scurrying with their whiskers in the ground.

One daughter had married a man the family considered beneath their standards. As a result, he was given only polite acceptance. The daughter reacted by stuffing anger under a polite exterior. A second daughter had been plagued with an eating disorder. The severity of the problem had been denied; it was time to own the fact she was anorexic. A third child, the son, had been actively gay for five years. Three of the family members had never noticed.

For that one day, at least, they all took their whiskers out of the ground and stopped and listened and noticed.

Jeremy, like the other mice in the village, stayed very busy, doing the things that mice do. He was always looking and searching, hurrying and scurrying, to and fro.

Mice work forty-hour, sixty-hour, eighty-hour weeks. Does that sound familiar? One self-acknowledged workaholic justified his schedule by saying, "Well, you do what you have to do!"

Mice tend to worry and scrutinize. Mice analyze and nitpick. At times, they become obsessive. They go over things again and again, and then one more time again, just to be sure. Sometimes this activity reflects a genuine expression of the inner self, but all too often the busyness is used to avoid dealing with the real concerns. We allow the innate conflicts of the conscious mind to drive us into activity. The busyness is displaced energy which perhaps would be better used were it directed to quiet the conscious mind, in order that we may hear the whisperings from the deeper self.

In time, we tend to become disconnected from our authentic selves. We lose touch with our spontaneity, playfulness, joy, imagination, and creativity. We lose our ability to be in the moment, and to experience wonder, sorrow, surprise, hope, vulnerability, love, and trust. In essence, we lose our connection with the Soul.

We identify, instead, with the ego self, that part of our identity which was shaped by parents, community, and culture. We become a reflection of the outside world. We are prompted by a false sense of duty and obligation and driven by a desperate emptiness which cries out to be filled with the approval and acceptance of others.

A scene from my childhood comes to mind. I remember a specific incident when my father discovered that we three children, Joanna, John, and I, had been sleighing down our sloping driveway, which led directly to the street. To emphasize his point about the dangers inherent in this kind of sledding, Dad called the three of us together to ask us each the same straightforward question: "What would you do if, when you got to the bottom of the hill, a vehicle came down the street?"

Joanna, the oldest, promptly answered, "I would lie real flat on the sled."

My father countered her response with, "You wouldn't have to worry about that. A car would make you flat, indeed!"

My brother was next. "I would roll off my sled," John said, with a confident look in his eyes. His statement got a definite nod of approval from Dad.

Now I, as the youngest of the three, had my turn. I didn't think I could give the same answer as John.

And surely Joanna had been off track. I was a such a careful little mouse (and safe answers are so very important to careful mice). After some hesitation, I said, "I am not sure," which was not the right answer at all!

The truth was that I knew exactly what to do. Just the week before this conversation, the exact situation which my father had anticipated had occurred. I had been sledding down the driveway, when suddenly, as I approached the bottom of the hill, a car quickly sped from around the corner and whizzed in front of the driveway. I rolled off the sled and managed to veer the unmanned sled away from the path of the car. In a moment of crisis, I had instinctively responded and averted danger. But when questioned later by my father, I was more concerned about the approval of others than I was in honoring my own truth.

Dad cautioned us to sled instead in a safer place, and the whole matter was dropped. No doubt, the incident has long been forgotten by all the other family members. But the memory stays with me because it signaled a theme which would later play out in my life in countless ways: seeking the courage to express feelings and thoughts without overconcern for pleasing others.

An even more challenging theme than being afraid to express thoughts and feelings is one of not even knowing what our thoughts and feelings are. Some of us have been so traumatized that we are still frozen in earlier experiences, cut off from our feeling and thinking reality.

Kari, a woman in Norway, recalls painful memories of the Nazi occupation of her small village during World War II. Before then, there had never been soldiers in her village; suddenly, with no explanation, soldiers arrived. Too many of them. Overnight, everything in her village changed. There was the eeriness of strangers in strange uniforms, speaking harsh words in guttural sounds her young ears could not understand. Kari remembers the clinking sounds of boots on pavement and the ever-prevailing presence of guns and weaponry. Ugly, giant machines were everywhere. Nothing felt safe anymore.

Her family and friends looked and talked and acted differently. There were worried looks and hushed voices, mumblings overheard late at night behind closed doors. There was scarcity. Not much food. Not much of anything. Adults had secrets. Many secrets. And children weren't told what they were. It was frightening, and no explanations were given. Kari's whole world changed. And she didn't know why.

The village had always been governed by a non-verbal consensus of what life was and how life was to be lived. Once that consensus was disturbed, fear gripped the village—not just the fear of what would happen under occupation, but the fear of not knowing what, collectively, to trust anymore.

One incident stands out above all the rest. It was twilight and the villagers gathered auspiciously on the bank of the river. Overhead, there were planes. So many planes. The whole sky was ablaze with light. Kari was terrified, and everyone else seemed to be afraid, too. She remembers her father picking her up and pointing frantically up to the sky. Then the bombing started. In the distance was the ugly, piercing sound of explosions ricocheting in the night. Much later, she learned that it was the night of the first Blitz, a devastating German air raid which affected much of Western Europe.

The night seemed to go on forever. She covered her ears and wanted to cover her eyes. Her father, in his well-meaning attempt to comfort her, told her how beautiful the sky was and that she should look at all the lights. What Kari needed was for him to tell her it was all right to be afraid. That he was frightened, too. War is terrifying for both adults and children. She needed to know that she could come to him when she felt apprehensive. She could talk to him and he would listen, and his love would make her feel safe. But he was too consumed with his own fears and too disturbed by the collective mania to be of any real comfort.

Instead, her father kept talking about the beautiful lights. Kari became afraid that who she was, as well as what she felt, was not acceptable. She tried to feel what he told her she "should" feel. She couldn't. She was a scared little mouse, paralyzed with fear. She became numb. No feelings.

Years later, Kari married an insensitive man. Her husband, as her father before, denied and controlled her feelings. She longed for children. She endured three miscarriages and four operations with no emotional support, and still, no baby. Her husband told her it wasn't hard. Still paralyzed in the frozen grief of her childhood, and still the scared little mouse, Kari obediently listened to what she "should" feel and, once again, numbed her feelings.

With the passage of time and with the help of extensive therapy, she is beginning, slowly, to trust her own thinking and feeling reality, even when it differs with that of others.

The Mousetrap Called "Consensus Reality"

Even without childhood trauma, how easy it is to allow ourselves to be governed by outer authority—the rules, beliefs, and opinions of others—without giving them our careful consideration. We accept what sociologists call "consensus reality," the reality agreed upon by most people as the way things "should" be.

If that consensus reality is one based on deep family, cultural, and spiritual values, we are likely to have an intrinsic sense of self and the confidence and courage to trust ourselves. If, on the other hand, that consensus reality is lacking in values, we may survive by dovetailing inconspicuously with the status quo. We obey the *shoulds* and *ought-tos* and *have-tos* which, in many cases, are blindly alluded to not so much because of their value, but because they exist. A grey dullness pervades. It becomes easier to blend in, to go along with what is, to be mediocre. We weigh and measure our responses, and in the process we become numb to our authentic selves, to genuine feelings and original thoughts. And then, years later, we one day find ourselves with the sobering awareness expressed so well by T.S. Eliot in *The Love Song of J. Alfred Prufrock*: "I have measured out my life with coffee spoons."

It may seem that an outer consensus reality does not rule us. But with careful scrutiny, we may discover we have internalized our consensus reality. Inside us, there may be a demanding, inner patriarch that keeps us stuck in Mouse Village just as effectively as any external pressure could ever do. We judge and criticize ourselves. We lavish guilt on ourselves because of our shortcomings. And we fall prey to limitations of family systems and generational patterns which we unconsciously perpetuate.

We may feel obliged to live out our parents' unlived lives, or we may feel trapped in roles assigned to us in our families of origin. Ann, for example, has an idealized view of her mother. She must "break the spell," as John Bradshaw so clearly puts it in his book *Creating Love*. Ann's mythologized view of her mother is that her mother sacrificed her life to give Ann the opportunity to be the ballerina she could never be. The truth is that her mother martyred herself, making Ann responsible for her own unlived life. Mom gave Ann opportunities but controlled her choices. As fate would have it, Ann grew too tall to fulfill the dream of becoming a ballerina. At fifty, there is a sad resignation that life somehow just happened. Because the child Ann didn't get to choose, the adult Ann has difficulty with the choices of everyday life. She doesn't trust herself. She doesn't know herself. She vacillates over decisions and second-guesses herself once choices are made. Her inner patriarch makes harsh demands. Since she failed to live her mother's dream, everything is on hold in her life. It is as though nothing can be enjoyed totally. Ann waits for permission to begin her dance of life.

Tom's inner patriarch is quite different than that of Ann's. He is governed by internal rules which keep him stuck in the same roles which were assigned to him as a child. As the youngest in a large family, Tom found his place by being funny and making everyone laugh. The very roles that once gave him power as a child now rob him of his identity as an adult. He has so over-identified with his role of clown and caretaker that much of his more authentic self has been discounted. As a man, he now seeks the purity of his deeper, more honest feelings.

We can live a lifetime as little mice, hurrying and scurrying, running to and fro with our whiskers in the ground, not really seeing very far, searching desperately for the self we never find. We can believe that this is how life was, how life is, and how life will always be. . .and so it is. . .just that. . .I call this living in Mouse Village. I believe all of us have lived there part of our lives. Some of us still do.

Many of us go back and forth from time to time. In fact, few of us have changed our permanent address.

Think about yourself and your Mouse Village. Be candid. Get a graphic picture of the scene. You might even be mildly amused. Describe yourself. What do you look like? How do you "busy" yourself? What are your feelings? Your thoughts? What beliefs dictate you and your Mouse Village? Take time to complete the sentence "When I am in Mouse Village, I. . ."

Hearing the Call

One day Jeremy began to hear a new strange sound, one he had not heard before. It was a roar coming from somewhere out in the distance. Now Jeremy was used to the sounds of the forest. He knew the different sounds of the two-legged and the four-legged and the winged and the hoofed. But this was unlike anything he had known.

Sometimes, he would stop everything and lift his head to the direction of the roar. He would strain to see what might be there, and he would wiggle his whiskers, hoping to sense something in the air. What could it be, he wondered?

And so Jeremy did what most of us do when we are not sure about something. He asked someone else. When we don't trust ourselves, we need confirmation from an outside source to validate our reality.

Jeremy scurried up to a fellow mouse and asked him, "Brother Mouse, do you hear a sound, a roaring in your ears?"

The other mouse didn't even bother to lift his whiskers out of the ground. He was too busy. "No, no, I don't hear anything. And besides, I don't have time

*to talk." And off he went before Jeremy had a chance
to say anything more.*

*Not to be easily discouraged, Jeremy decided to
ask another mouse the same question. Maybe this
mouse had heard the sound.*

*The second mouse looked at him in a most peculiar
way. "Sound? What sound?" And before Jeremy could
stop him long enough to describe what he had heard,
the second mouse scampered off, disappearing behind
the pines.*

The sound which Jeremy heard comes from the
Unknown. It is the voice of Spirit, the Higher Self,
the Inner Voice. It communicates to us in a number
of ways: a hunch, a feeling that persists, a revealing
dream, an inner knowing, an intuitive flash, a chance
meeting which has particular relevance, an experience
that has metaphorical significance, or a sensing that
defies the rational process. We can experience any
number of these "calls," even within the course of
a single day. For life is always calling to us, even
though we may not always hear that call.

Sometimes, the call from our inner world is confirmed with an experience in the outer world. It is
those moments of exquisite synchronicity that serve
to keep us in awe of life. Gina, in England, recalls
an experience in which her inner and outer worlds
converged in a most meaningful way. She was sitting
on her bed reading a letter from her ex-boyfriend,
painfully reviewing what had been a most difficult
relationship, one in which she found herself continually
longing and hoping for more connection, more commitment. It was a futile wish for the improbable, a
fantasy built on a dream of what might be, rather
than a realistic view of what was. The letter was
his final exit, although in many ways he had never
entered the relationship.

As Gina read the letter, she glanced up to see a butterfly trapped inside her bedroom window, struggling to free itself. As it fluttered unsuccessfully against the glass, she was reminded of the many times she had struggled for a sense of self but felt trapped in her willingness to endure unnecessary hardship and pain. As she finished the final words of the letter, simultaneously the butterfly found its way to freedom. A resonating rush of energy surged through her body. The butterfly served as a powerful metaphor. It was the call to give up her pleasing-passive role, a childhood pattern learned early to gain approval from disinterested parents and one which she continued in relationship after relationship. It was time to free herself and take flight.

The sound of the inner voice has a distinctive quality, like no other voice we may hear. A mother can distinguish her child's voice amid the voices of a hundred other children on a busy playground. She knows her child's voice because she has listened to it countless times. Likewise, the more we listen to our inner voice, the more certainty there is in distinguishing the sound of the true self from all the other voices that may be crying out to be heard (the voice of ego, the voice of fear, the voice of anger, etc.). And the more we listen to the inner voice, the more it speaks to us.

At first, the call comes in a gentle fashion. We may have a dream, for example. And there may be an incident in our outer world which parallels the message from the dream. We listen to the dream, notice the metaphor in relationship to what is occurring around us, and make the necessary changes. But when we ignore or discount those messages, the communication becomes more faint. The voice becomes less frequent, less distinct. It is as though our Higher Self ceases its struggle to get through to our denser reality. We forgo the option of conscious choice, and life becomes the tough taskmaster. Instead of gentleness, we are given the "divine boot," kicked out of our complacency or resistance into difficult challenges which demand change. There may be illness, loss, separation, or other trauma, experiences which serve to wake us up to a deeper reality.

There are many kinds of authentic calls. On a practical level, the call may be the impulse to respond to a want ad in the newspaper, a strong feeling that propels you to re-connect with a friend you haven't seen in years, or a sudden knowing that it is time to make a geographical change, go back to school, change jobs, or end a relationship.

Or the call may be of another kind altogether. A particular story or poem might call out to you. A particular area of the world may call you to come visit or even to make a geographical move. Creative self-expression may suddenly beckon. Grandma Moses didn't begin painting until she was in her eighties!

We may, at times, sense the unspoken call from another person. A stirring story is one about Suzanne, who talked long-distance to her friend one Sunday afternoon, as was her custom. There was nothing distinctive or particularly different about that conversation to alert her in any way to any special concern for her friend. Later that night, however, she found herself dialing the number of her friend again. There was no logical reason to call, since she had already talked to her that day. Suzanne was startled at her own reflexive action, but continued to dial anyway. This time when her friend answered, her speech was heavy and slurred. Suzanne sensed what had happened. Her friend had overdosed on pills. Immediately, she dialed 911, an action which saved her friend's life.

From another perspective, a call may beckon the hero or heroine to a quest, an undertaking, a mission, or a journey. These calls, which come from the very depths of your being, enlist you in mythic tasks: to pursue a lifetime dream, to serve in some capacity, to undertake some historical undertaking, or to follow a spiritual pursuit. For example, Orville and Wilbur Wright answered the call to adventure. They dared to explore new horizons with their contributions in the field of aerodynamics. President Clinton's story about the impact of his meeting with John F. Kennedy is an example of a call to public service. Or the call may come from nature. There may be the sudden impulse to mountain trek in Tibet or river raft in Colorado.

The call, of course, need not literally be a sound, as it was for Jeremy, for the murmurings of the heart make their voices heard in a variety of ways. But the fact that Jeremy heard a sound is significant. Sound demands attention. As David A. Cooper states, "Certain sounds evoke deep stirring in the unconscious realms, stimulating mysterious and powerful urges that transcend intellectual concepts. These are sounds that lure us into the domain of the sacred."

In many of the ancient traditions, sound is used to awaken the individual. The sound is a call to Spirit. Sikhs blow blasts of a trumpet to announce the arrival of the Holy Granth, their sacred text. Muslims sound the vocal call to prayer: *Allah Hu Akhnar* ("God is most great"). Christian worship often begins with bells, the chords of an organ, the voices of a choir. In the Jewish tradition, the blowing of the shofar, the ram's horn, is the call to prayer. And shamans and other spiritual healers use rattles, chants, whistles, bells, howls, grunts, and other sounds.

The call that Jeremy hears is the call of Spirit, or what is known in many traditions as a Sacred Call. It is the call of the True Self, which calls out, from deep within, to be recognized as our true identity. The false self, the ego, the "I," made up of the thoughts and reactions that we have allowed to rule our lives, is no longer in charge. Each time we experience a Sacred Call, we are instantly drawn into our true nature, which Joseph Campbell describes as "that interior, ineffable source of being, consciousness, and bliss."

What distinguishes a Sacred Call from any other kind of call? According to Cooper, "The Sacred call is transformative. When such a call occurs and we hear it—really hear it—our shift to higher consciousness is assured. A decision is made and a turn in direction is taken. The one who receives the message recognizes a new sense of reality, and follows, as if by intuition, in a way that may elude verbal explanation."

Leaving Mouse Village

When none of the other mice knew anything about the sound, Jeremy decided that the best thing he could do would be to forget about the whole thing and get busy. He knew how to be a busy little mouse. And so he started hurrying and scurrying to and fro once more.

But no matter how busy he was, he would still hear the sound. He tried to pretend that it had disappeared. But even when he tried not to hear it, he knew it was still there!

Jeremy became more and more curious about the sound. So one day, he decided to go off by himself and investigate. It was easy to scurry off from the other mice. They were too busy to notice he had gone, anyway.

When he was off by himself, the sound was stronger and much clearer. Now he could sit quietly and listen hard.

Heeding the call heralds a moment of spiritual passage, a dying to the old and birth of the new, the mystery of transformation. The familiar life horizon has been outgrown, and the old concepts, ideals, and emotional patterns no longer fit; the time for the passing of a threshold is at hand. Leaving Mouse Village marks the shift from an identity with the unauthentic self, dictated by consensus reality, the reality most people accept, to an identity instead with the authentic self, the central point within the psyche to which everything is related. The departure is not without its anxiety. For, as Freud has suggested, all moments of separation and new birth produce anxiety similar to the original birth trauma and separation from the mother.

Leaving Mouse Village has two requirements. The first requirement is the courage to venture into the unknown. How many times do we have a strong intuition but fail to follow it, either because we don't trust that feeling enough or we don't have the courage to follow what we feel?

There is an often-told story about a woman who loses a key. She stands under a brightly lit lamp post and searches for it there. A stranger comes by and asks her what she is looking for.

"I am looking for my lost key."

"Oh," he replies. "Did you lose it here under the lamp post?"

"No, I lost it down there," she answers, pointing to the darkness ahead, "but I can't see there."

To find the symbolic key, we must be willing to go from the known into the unknown, with no guarantees, no assurances, no certainty of where our venture into the unknown might lead.

I am reminded of an earlier period in my life when I first moved to Virginia Beach. My seventeen-year marriage was over. I had left a comfortable life, a large home appointed with beautiful antiques situated on four acres on the James River, and the accompanying lifestyle that goes with being married to a professional and doing all the "right things." The decision to leave had clearly been mine, but the consequences of that choice had not been squarely faced. I was left reeling from the aftermath of having exchanged safety for uncertainty. The abrupt and drastic changes in lifestyle left me overwhelmed and burdened with too many choices. My life had taken on a surrealistic overtone. The truth is I was terrified.

I called a dear friend in New York, a seventy-plus "young" woman to seek her sage advice to deal with what I was experiencing as my great travail. "Suzanne, I don't know what I am going to do, or even where I am going to live."

I was totally unprepared for her response. "How fascinating!" she exclaimed. "I will have to try that some time!" So much for my sob story! I started to chuckle. Thanks to Suzanne, I was jolted into seeing my situation from quite a different perspective. It was the push I needed to move out of my limbo and to begin facing the unknown with affirmative action, by making conscious decisions about my new life in Virginia Beach. Travesty or opportunity, the choice was mine!

A willingness to venture into the unknown is one thing. Successfully confronting the mythic task of "leaving home" is quite another. Both are required if we are to successfully leave Mouse Village. Leaving home does not necessarily refer to a geographical move, for we can move geographically but remain in a limited awareness. Leaving home means severing the umbilical cord to all that prevents us from experiencing our true identity.

In many of the ancient myths and legends, there are three underlying segments around which a story is woven: leaving home, facing challenges, and returning home. The hero (or, of course, heroine) may leave home voluntarily, as in the case of Jeremy, to go off to a foreign land on some quest or adventure. Or he may be cast out from his homeland for any one of a variety of reasons. Next, the hero must face his challenges, or aspects of self, mirrored in the people and experiences he meets along the way. By people, we include monsters, demons, witches, trolls, animals, tricksters, helpers, guardians, etc. Finally, there is the return home. The hero, having met the various aspects of self, returns home. It is not necessarily the literal home to which the hero returns, but "home" in the metaphorical sense of returning to the real self.

In the more ancient traditions, rites of passage served to help those crossing difficult thresholds of transformation. The ceremonies were concrete metaphors that severed conscious and unconscious patterns and then introduced the participants to the forms and feelings of the new stage.

Our modern world provides few such opportunities for these kinds of experiences. However, the need for support in making life transitions is evidenced in the number and variety of support groups which have sprung up everywhere. These groups often provide the deep interpersonal connection which were formerly found in family and community. Sometimes, these groups include ceremonies of various kinds to ritualize major life transitions and to celebrate both the beginning and the ending of significant cycles.

A meaningful ceremony for me is the Drum Dance, a three-day, dry-fast dance, held annually in locations both in the United States and Europe under the guidance of Joseph Rael. The Dance contains the three essential elements for any ceremony: movement, sound, and purpose (or intent). In this particular ceremony, the movement is the dance itself, a metaphor for the expansion of light; the sound, the beat of the drum, takes one deep into the inner self; and the purpose for the Dance is personal as well as planetary healing. Although the experience for each participant is unique, one thing is assured: at the completion of the Dance, every dancer is in a different place inwardly than when he began. The very nature of dance expands the psyche, severing conscious and unconscious patterns. Just the act of participating in the Dance automatically causes a shift in consciousness.

At times, the Dance is physically grueling. Somehow, you endure and wait for those resounding moments of triumph, those exquisite moments when you know you have danced through and beyond some blockage. In that moment, you are lifted into stillness where you are no longer dancing; instead, you are *being danced.* Your feet become the drumstick and the Earth the drum. You slip into those spaces "where God hides," in Rael's words, and, for a lingering moment, you touch the transcendent.

Whether or not you choose to use a ceremony to facilitate making a shift in consciousness is purely a personal matter. What is imperative, if you are to "leave home," is that you separate from the mosaic of identities you have settled for and begin, instead, to trust the true self.

Saying Goodbye to Other Mice

When we stand ready to cross the threshold and leave Mouse Village, we review the people and experiences in our lives. We place the people and events in our lives with a new perspective by beginning to understand their deeper significance. We relinquish judgment and become gentle with ourselves and with others.

If you have ever examined the underside of a homemade quilt, you are struck by what seems to be a hodge-podge of knots, hanging threads, and raw edges. How could anything beautiful be made from such randomness and confusion? But when you turn the quilt over, you see a beautiful, intricate, delicate pattern. Each piece is an integral part of the whole design. Each piece is placed deliberately in relationship to the other pieces. Placing people and events in your life is rather like turning a guilt over to the right side. You begin to see how each part of your life is an integral part of a far grander design.

Pamela, a woman in England, received a letter from her former husband that stirred a whole range of feelings. After many years of estrangement, receiving a letter from her ex was a mixed blessing. Years before, when she was in her early forties, he had left her for another woman. At the time, it was a devastating experience. He was her world, her Renaissance man, accomplished in the world of finance, involved in humanitarian concerns, and recognized as a connoisseur of art. In addition, he was her best friend and constant companion and was dashingly handsome, energetic, passionate, and sensitive. She had lived life with him and through him. Without him, all seemed empty.

Life had booted her out of Mouse Village. At forty-plus, she was forced to go back to school to earn a degree and begin a career. And so she did, at first with great effort, then with great success. The world of art, to which her former husband had introduced her, changed from being a world she could only appreciate in a detached way to becoming her world, her own place of unique expression.

In retrospect, all of her years of struggle seemed somewhat remote, for she had gained depth and definition through it all. Now, as a mature woman, she enjoyed a "significant other" relationship, a supportive and interesting circle of friends, a successful and meaningful career, and a comfortable home.

In sharp contrast, the letter from her ex spoke of loneliness (the relationship with the younger woman had long ago ended), of ill-health, of changes in finance, and of estrangement from their children. He was leading a life of quiet desperation. At an earlier time, she would have felt triumph, a sense that in the end she had won. But no such feelings surfaced. Instead, there was a sense of deep compassion, of wanting to see him one last time, to somehow place him in her life and to acknowledge all he had been for her.

They had first met on the River Seine. It seemed appropriate that their final meeting be there as well, at the familiar café, to sit together once again and share a bottle of Chardonnay. She wanted to thank him for being the one who had given her children, for opening her eyes to art and beauty, for being the most passionate lover in her life, and for the special moments that transcend words. For all of this, she was thankful. And even his leaving had, in retrospect, been a gift, for she had learned, in time, to love and trust herself. At any rate, a toast and a fond farewell. . .

Once we place the people and events in our lives, we are no longer restricted by our history; we are empowered, instead, by a deeper understanding and a sense of honor about our past.

Jeremy stood on the edge of Mouse Village and took one long look back at the only life he had ever known. He sat listening to the sound for a long time, and he knew he could no longer be content to just listen. It was time to discover more about this sound. He turned to face another direction. He looked out into the darkness of the vast unknown and boldly left Mouse Village.

CHAPTER TWO
Leap of Faith

*J*eremy was listening hard to the sound in the distance, when suddenly he heard someone say, *"Hello, Little Brother."* Jeremy was so startled he almost ran away. *"Hello,"* again said the voice. *It sounded friendly enough.*

"Who are you?" asked the timid little mouse.

"It is I, Brother Raccoon. You are all by yourself, Little Brother," said the raccoon. *"What are you doing here all alone?"*

Jeremy was embarrassed. He didn't want to have to talk to anybody about the sound. Especially not after what happened in Mouse Village.

"I heard a sound," he said timidly. *"A roaring in my ears and I am investigating it."*

"A roaring in your ears? You mean the River," said the raccoon, without any hesitation. *"Come, walk with me. I will take you there."*

Reflections From the River of Life

Jeremy was amazed! No sooner had he ventured out of Mouse Village than immediately he met someone who not only knew the sound in the distance but would take him to its source! Jeremy was determined to find out once and for all what this sound was about.

"Once I find out about this River, I can go back to my work and my life in Mouse Village," thought Jeremy. "Why, I will even ask Raccoon to return with me. If the mice in the village don't believe me, they will surely believe a raccoon."

Little Mouse walked close behind the raccoon, so as to be sure not to lose his way. His heart was pounding. He had never known such excitement. They wound their way through a cathedral forest of tall evergreens. There was an intoxicating smell of pine and cedar. As they drew closer to the River, the sound became louder. There was a sense that something important was about to happen. The air became cooler, and there was a fine mist. Suddenly, they came to the River! The mighty River! It was so huge that Little Mouse could not see across it. And it roared, loudly, rushing swiftly on its course, coming from some other place, going to the great unknown.

For one long, sacred moment, Jeremy was one with the river. He watched the river in reverent silence, inspired by its awesome beauty and the mesmerizing sounds. Western cosmology begins with, "And God said, Let there be light." God created light with his own voice—with sound—signifying that sound is the essential matter of the universe. Sound touches us deeply. It nourishes our most primal needs and reassures us, keeping us in harmony with life. Certain sounds, such as the roar of the river, evoke deep stirrings in the unconscious realms. These sounds, according to David A. Cooper, call to us in soulful ways that "stimulate mysterious and powerful urges and transcend intellectual concepts."

A friend recalls a peak experience when just hearing the pure sound of the river was a much-needed healing balm. Like Jeremy, he experienced a timeless moment when he became one with the river. John had made a trip to San Diego to reconnect with a female friend, hoping to build a permanent relationship. His dream soon turned into bitter disappointment. It was clear that any long-term relationship with her was simply not to be. To find solace from his pain, he sought refuge in an enchanted spot which he often visited in National Park, San Diego. It was a remote place where he could stretch out on a large river stone and comfortably lie, sometimes for hours, transfixed by the roar and rush of water cascading over rocks. In this secluded spot, a diverse group of onlookers would regularly congregate. Here, differences would disappear. Each person would sense which special stone was his and claim it as a private sanctuary. The one commonality was the shared reverence for the river.

To my friend John, the art of listening to the sound of the river is a high form of Zen meditation, a way to slip into the gaps and go beyond time. On this particular day, he lay on a rock by the river in a total state of bliss, completely absorbed by sound. What seemed more like five minutes extended into five hours and left him wondering, later, where time had gone. The sound lifted him out of his emotional pain and restored his Soul. He regained his equilibrium and was able to satisfactorily complete the relationship with his friend instead of slipping back into old abandonment issues. His experience with sound made him keenly aware that he had been neglecting his inner self; as a result, he made a commitment to designate time each day for meditation. The sonorous sound of the river called him back to himself.

An interesting point in our story is that the mouse went to a river. If Jeremy had gone to a mountain instead of a river, he would have begun to climb, for mice can maneuver in earth. But mice can't manage in water. His mouse self was rendered helpless before something he was unable to manipulate and master. He could only surrender to the song of the river and listen to its many voices, which together make up the music of life.

When we live in Mouse Village, our identity is determined by who and what others tell us we are. Once we look in the River, we no longer need to depend exclusively on the opinion of others for self-knowledge. The River of Life gives us a more profound way of knowing ourselves. The River, which is Life, is a mirror. The people, the situations, the symbols in our life merely reflect inner aspects of self. The mirrors in our outer world reveal messages we would otherwise not be able to hear.

When we look in the River of Life, we begin to see our inner selves. We begin to take responsibility for our underlying issues which determine why we attract certain people and particular situations in our lives. In time, we can detect our weaknesses, the aspects of self we are most afraid of, reflected in life around us. We see our greatest strengths mirrored and face those fears as well. What would happen if we claimed all our power? What would happen if we allowed ourselves to be all that we are? What would happen if we did not undermine or sabotage ourselves?

When we listen attentively to the many voices of the River, as did Jeremy and John, in time we may discover the oneness in it all and realize that the voices in the River belong to each other. We no longer distinguish the merry voice from the weeping voice, or the childish voice from the manly voice, or the lament of those who yearn from the laughter of the wise. All the voices are interwoven and interlocked, entwined in a thousand ways. All of them together are the world.

We enter that transcendent state of oneness, described so poetically by Herman Hesse in *Siddhartha*.

When he listened to this river. . .to this song of a thousand voices: when he did not listen to the sorrow or laughter, when he did not bind his soul to any one particular voice and absorb it in himself, but heard them all, the whole, the unity; then the great song of a thousand voices consisted of one word: Om-perfection.

"It's powerful!" the little mouse said, fumbling for words.

"Yes, the river is a great thing," answered Raccoon, "but here, let me introduce you to a friend."

In a smoother, shallower place was a lily pad, bright and green. Sitting upon it was a frog, almost as green as the pad it sat on. The frog's white belly stood out clearly.

"Hello, Little Brother," said the frog. "Welcome to the river."

"I must leave you now," cut in Raccoon, "but do not fear, Little Brother, for Frog will care for you now."

The Role of the Raccoon, the Guide

As soon as the raccoon completes his task of guiding Jeremy to the River, he leaves quietly, unnoticed. He will return to the edge of Mouse Village and await the next person who needs a guide to the River. It may be a long wait, for few have the courage to venture out of Mouse Village. But when the next seeker crosses the threshold, leaving the confines of the village behind, the raccoon will willingly serve as a guide to whomever it might be. True teachers have no preferences. The raccoon gladly took Jeremy to the river. The truth is he would have taken anyone who was interested. But then, no one else had asked.

Raccoons are midwives who assist in the birth of consciousness. Although the role of the midwife is critical, the focus is the birth, not the midwife. Once the birth process is complete, the midwife is often forgotten. As soon as the raccoon safely delivered Jeremy to the River, he appropriately averted Jeremy's attention away from himself and his role as a guide and directed attention, instead, toward the next phase in the mouse's journey. The raccoon's timing was impeccable. He knew when his task with Jeremy was complete. He sensed when to introduce Jeremy to the frog and when to slip away unobtrusively.

All animals, including raccoons, represent the instinctual self. Meeting with the raccoon was also an indication that the little mouse was coming face-to-face with his own instinctual self and was beginning to trust inner impulses.

Jeremy was indeed fortunate that his particular guide was a raccoon. For it is the unique nature of raccoons to wash everything they eat in water. They wash in the River of Life and they understand its mysteries. What they take into their physical, emotional, mental, and spiritual bodies is purified, or washed in water (or light). Raccoons have no need for control, no need for adulation, and no attachment to outcome.

No limit is placed on the number of Raccoons we can have in our journey. And our Raccoons need not only be people. Raccoons can be turning-point experiences which can appear in any number of forms. A book, for example, can appear at a critical juncture and serve as a guide to the next stage of our journey. But no matter how many Raccoons we may have, the experience with our first Raccoon is always a cherished memory.

One of my first significant Raccoons was a book entitled *There is a River*, written by Thomas Sugrue. It is a story of a transpersonal explorer, Edgar Cayce, who shed light on other lifetimes and other realities. The book was a Raccoon waiting on my path, ready to take me to the River. It came during a period of deep introspection when I was exploring answers to some rather perplexing philosophical questions. The material from the Cayce readings clarified previously unanswered spiritual questions and confirmed the validity of many of my personal experiences. The book was life-changing. My entire perception of reality shifted. (There is nothing so strange as the way the strangeness wears off the strange.)

Pause a moment and reflect on a significant Raccoon in your life. Who was that person and/or experience waiting on your path once you left Mouse Village? In what way did that Raccoon guide you into the next phase of your journey?

Leap of Faith

"Who are you?" Jeremy asked.

"Why, I am a frog."

"A frog?" questioned Jeremy. He had never seen a frog before. "How is it possible to be so far out in the mighty river?"

"That is very easy," said the little frog. "I can go both on land and on water. And I can live both above the water and below in the water. I am the Keeper of the Water."

Jeremy was astonished! He tried to think of words. But no words came. He had never met the Keeper of the Water.

Without hesitating, the frog said, "Little Mouse, would you like some Medicine Power?"

"Medicine Power? Do you mean for me? Yes, of course. What do I do?" asked the eager little mouse.

"It is not that hard. All you need to do is crouch down real low and jump up as high as you can."

"That's all?" asked Jeremy.

"Yes. Crouch down as low as you can and jump up as high as you can! That will give you your medicine!"

Little Mouse did exactly what the frog told him to do. He crouched down as low as he could and jumped as high as he could. And when he did, his eyes saw something even more powerful than the mighty River. He saw the Sacred Mountain.

The jump that Jeremy took is what is known as the Leap of Faith. Faith is an unquestioning trust in someone or something. In this case, Jeremy trusted the frog. And what the frog told him was that if he wanted his power, he would need to leap. He had to go beyond himself, take new risks, move beyond limited perceptions and beliefs of who and what he was, to experience new levels of consciousness. Growth is a continuum that spirals upwards. A leap of faith, on the other hand, is an awakening characterized by a quantum shift in consciousness.

When Jeremy made his leap, he saw the Sacred Mountain, which is even more compelling than the River. The Mountain is the Heart of God. When we see the Mountain, we are stirred by that which is sacred to us, by that which has depth and genuineness. To see the Mountain is to connect with the Soul, to be nourished by what we feel and know and dream.

We begin to remember our real selves. We remember our spontaneity, playfulness, joy, imagination, creativity, and the ability to be in the moment. We awaken new possibilities. We remember our ability to experience wonder, sorrow, surprise, hope, love, and trust.

A young man made a spiritual pilgrimage to the Southwest to visit the Anasazi ruins. The decision to make the trip was definitely a leap of faith. He was at a critical juncture in his life, a time in which personal decisions were delayed until he sorted out his relationship with his father. Alan knew he couldn't be like his father, nor could he be who his father wanted him to be. And it would be futile to continue in his rebellious stage, acting out with drugs and alcohol. Instead of freedom, these addictions brought more despair and left him with a deeper sense of helplessness.

The sacred land of the Southwest had called him in some mysterious way and he had responded. Deciding to take the trip wasn't a logical decision; it meant putting his education on hold and spending his last bit of hard-earned money. But it seemed necessary. Alan trusted what he felt. When we are willing to make a giant leap into the unknown, as did the little mouse and this young man, we open ourselves to mountaintop experiences.

Three months later, Alan found himself exploring the ancient ruins of the Anasazi Indians in Bandelier, New Mexico. Perhaps he was feeling, at some non-verbal level, the need to search out ancient roots and, in so doing, search out his own roots.

Exploring the ruins was a somber experience. He sensed the silent wisdom of the Ancient Ones and the blessings being passed on, somehow, to those fortunate enough to walk time-worn pathways of sacred land. At such places, the invisible energy fields and the tangible worlds interface. The effect on the psyche is nonverbal and most profound.

Needing quiet time to reflect, Alan decided to hike up a nearby mountain. What this young man did not know was that, in the Native American tradition, vision questers traditionally go to a mountaintop. Symbolically, they enter the center of the Medicine Wheel, which is the Heart of God.

Once on the mountaintop, Alan noticed a circular design in the ground. Someone who was there before him had carefully chosen stones and meticulously placed them to form a perfect circle in the earth. It seemed that this Medicine Wheel was waiting just for him. It was a gift from Spirit and an auspicious opportunity for personal ceremony. He reverently entered the circle and sat directly in its center. He said prayers to honor the four directions, the East (mental), the South (emotional), the West (physical), and the North (spiritual). Before him was an exquisite panorama of desert beauty. The artist in him wanted to seize the moment. He reached for his camera and was concentrating on loading film when, all of a sudden, a large bird whooshed over his head so close he could feel the wind from the flap of its wings. He was startled! It took him a moment to collect himself before he could follow the magnificent bird with his eyes. He could identify it, now. . .a giant golden eagle! He watched it soar majestically, making a wide circle, and then, as though to make a definitive statement, the eagle completed the circle and flew breathtakingly close over his head once again.

To this young man, all life is a metaphor of the mind of God. The deeper significance of this event would not go unnoticed. It was significant to him that an eagle, a metaphor for Great Spirit, flew from the East, the place where wisdom enters. He knew Great Spirit would give him wisdom and it be would forthcoming. This was a moment of deep communion with his Soul. He had reclaimed himself. Tears streamed down his face. He could feel his heart and all within him that was authentic, connected, powerful, and real. Simultaneously, he knew his relationship with his father would no longer be a paralyzing issue. He could cease the struggle of seeking his identity through conflict with his father. Instead, he could boldly step into his life and move toward his goals which, heretofore, had been delayed. He had a renewed trust in Great Spirit. He was assured now that he would be given the strength he needed to live out his dream. When he came down from the mountain, his eyes glistened. This mountain would always be his mountain, his place for reclaiming his power.

Once we glimpse our Mountain, in the symbolic sense, as did the little mouse and the young man in New Mexico, we have an inextricable sense of who we are. Even if our view of the Mountain is fleeting and the experience is momentary, we are empowered to trust our inner truth, and to honor what we feel and know and dream.

We do not necessarily need to go anywhere physically to experience the leap of faith. Eric Butterworth, a well-known Unity minister, tells a story about one man's shift in consciousness which occurred while he was simply sitting in a chair! The man, who was a middle-aged, middle-management executive, similar in many ways to many other men, was suddenly given his final notice. The company which had employed him for twenty-some years was downsizing and there was no longer a position for him. The news was devastating. At his age, job marketability was not promising. Not only that, but he had three children, two of whom were college-age. There were educational costs, mortgage payments, car payments, etc., to consider. He was stunned! He had never anticipated or planned for anything like this. He sat staring blankly into nowhere. He could not move. When office hours were over, he continued to sit and stare. Numb. Overwhelmed.

As he sat staring into nothingness, suddenly a tiny spider caught his attention. It was hanging on a thread hooked in at the ceiling and inching his way downwards, very close to the man's desk. At a certain point, the spider began meticulously to spin a web.

The man had never watched a web in process. It was fascinating. Minuscule silvery threads were magically being woven into an intricate design. Suddenly, he felt an empathetic connection between himself and the spider. Like the spider, he was hanging on a thread. If a divine intelligence is able to communicate with a spider and let it know how to spin a web with such perfection, then surely he could trust that same intelligence to guide his life. He started thinking about all the things he had really wanted to do but had postponed. Writing, for example. He had been so busy being "responsible" that his creativity had been pushed aside. Other options and possibilities came to mind. He could begin reclaiming important parts of himself he had previously disowned. He began to experience a glimmer of hope. His life could have so much more depth and value. It was a leap of faith to consider the possibility of living like the spider, to be in the moment, to listen, to trust, and to know that he would be given the knowledge to weave his own unique design.

Rediscover the Sacred Mountain

When Joseph Campbell was asked by someone in an audience what he should do with his life, the reply was the oft-quoted, "Young man, follow your bliss." Certainly, the advice from Campbell is sage wisdom. The difficulty, however, lies in knowing what our "bliss" is. How can we catch a glimpse of our Sacred Mountain, even if it is only for a fleeting look? How can we touch, taste, sense, feel, re-awaken, re-kindle, stir, remember, that which is sacred within us? How can we tap our intuitive source of spirituality and wisdom and be nourished by what we feel and know and dream?

Certainly, life itself can provide the catalysts we need to enable us to see the Sacred Mountain. Such was the case for Jeremy, for the young man in the Southwest, and for the middle-aged executive. Life is the indisputable teacher and is capable of creating the precise situation needed for us to return to our deeper selves. But is it possible to see the Sacred Mountain without the need for external events to catapult us into shifting to our more soulful selves?

Over the years, I have been privileged to be present during the sharing of the diverse life stories of many people throughout the world. Those stories are told in a variety of ways. They may be dramatized, drawn in spontaneous drawings, molded in clay, or expressed verbally. As I look and listen to each story with a particular interest in appreciating its sacredness, I am struck by some remarkable similarities. It would seem that during childhood, all of us, without exception, have had at least one moment in which we felt connected to the divine, although we may not always consciously remember the experience. For it is in childhood, when we are most innocent, that God's thumbprint is indelibly imprinted on our souls.

I find that these early experiences can be placed in three distinct categories. In the first category are the fortunate few who have had experiences in childhood so compelling that they never lost their connection with the sacred dimension of life. Eileen and Aaron are examples of persons who undoubtedly belong in that first group.

Eileen recalls the first years of her life when she heard the heavenly sounds of celestial music four or five times a day. What she heard defies the parameters of language's ability to adequately describe, for these sounds originate in another dimension of reality. Eileen describes the music as an ethereal blend of tinkling bells, each varied in tone and pitch, accompanied by the lilting sounds of harps and other stringed instruments; it was indeed heavenly music! Eileen could hear those delicate sounds more easily when it was quiet and she was alone. For in solitude the veil between this third dimension and the higher dimensions lifts somewhat. In particular, Eileen could hear the music while sitting alone eating, or walking down the sidewalk, or before drifting off to sleep at night. And in those quiet times Eileen would be comforted, as God and all His angels would sing, especially for her.

Although different in nature to the childhood experiences of Eileen, Aaron's early memories are equally compelling. Aaron describes his first childhood memory as one in which he was on the ceiling in his bedroom, looking down at himself, a tiny infant in a crib. According to Aaron, he spent a great deal of his time as a child in an out-of-body state. Not only was he able to move in and out of his physical body, but he was able to see auras, or the colors, shapes, and images around a person, and to accurately interpret those symbols.

In the second category of special childhood experiences, the persons felt a connection to the sacred dimension of life, but their experiences were discounted. They were either denied, ridiculed, or criticized by those around them. Or they minimized their experiences themselves because they were afraid to trust their own truth.

Persons in the third group have no conscious memory of any special moments in their early years. Their childhoods were so soul-severing because of trauma or abuse that they feel permanently disconnected from any loving Source of life. With help, they can be assisted into recalling or at least imagining one pleasant moment.

One way to reconnect with our Sacred Mountain is to revisit magical moments from your childhood by recalling childhood experiences when you felt loved, or joyful, inspired, happy, carefree, whimsical, creative, playful, safe, etc. Any number of incidents might come to mind, incidents which might appear to be insignificant. For example, you might recall the heavenly scent of jasmine on a hot summer night, or baking gingerbread with grandmother in the kitchen, or watching the play of light on treetops, or making costumes out of crepe paper with a best friend, or daydreaming under a giant oak tree. These experiences may seem trivial, but they have significance because they are selectively recalled and because they are scenes, or moments, which stir mysterious chords of memory. Within those memories are important clues which reveal that which, for you, is sacred in life. Those experiences often foreshadow a life's work, an avocation, a call to serve in a particular way (as opposed to a vocation, which may simply be a job to produce income). Most important, you learn what gives life meaning, that which calls uniquely to you. With a bit of creative detective work, you can decipher metaphors and draw inferences which could give important clues to your deeper nature.

An artist recalls a early scene when, as a two-year-old, he silently took his aunt by the hand and ceremoniously walked her over to stand with him, reverently, in front of a brightly lit Christmas tree, decorated with balls of every color. Years later his art would simulate that early imprint. His artistic signature would be his ability to skillfully reflect the play of light amid brilliant color.

Jean's special childhood moment was a time when she danced on the sidewalk to the nodding approval of her adoring grandfather. It was not necessarily that life was calling her to be a dancer, but it was affirming her innate ability to create her own unique movement in life. As a woman, she would need to call on her dancing spirit, her creativity, spontaneity, and liveliness, to weather some demanding challenges. It is interesting to note that now, as a therapist, she has added arrhythmic movement to her repertoire, teaching others to be at ease with their movement in life.

The father of a well-known minister, whom we will call Caleb, recalls an experience when his son did not come home from first grade at his normal time. It was at least an hour past the scheduled time when his son returned home to the father who was now very concerned. Caleb very matter-of-factly explained that one of his classmates had forgotten how to get home, and there was no parent to assist. Caleb knew the way and so he took his friend Lauren by the hand and walked her home. Later in life, he would know how to take many people "home."

Whether or not we choose to explore the symbolism of special childhood moments as a way to explore our own sacred dimensions, no doubt life will present additional opportunities which will serve to reconnect us with our Sacred Mountain. The experience can be one of a transcendent nature, a vivid dream, an out-of-body experience, an experience with light or sound, etc.; or we can be awakened by experiences on the opposite end of the paradigm—by death, loss, pain, struggle, hardship, etc. In either case, we have the opportunity to surrender to an unseen reality and reclaim the real self.

An example of a woman who is awakened through facing and overcoming obstacles is beautifully presented in the compelling story "Weaver of Worlds," by David Jongeward. In the story, Carolyn Jongeward accompanies her husband David, an archeologist, into Navaho country while he does writing and research. At first she watches with mild curiosity as the Navaho women weave their Javah. In time, Carolyn becomes intrigued with the weaving of the Navaho women, who are the recognized masters in this ancient art form. She develops a strong desire to learn the ancient ways and asks to be taught, not knowing what she is really asking.

Thus begins a story of initiation, an intense inner journey which is paralleled by a demanding outer journey. At times Carolyn's teachers treat her with kindness and teach her with patience. At other times, she is laughed at, ignored, ridiculed, and shamed. She is given a decrepit loom which frequently breaks down, not told how to thread her loom, given old rotting threads which break easily, and made to clean up the hogan while others casually sit sipping Coca-Cola and leafing through catalogues. She experiences anger, resentment, frustration, and many tears. Carolyn struggles to deal with her inner turmoil; meanwhile, her apprenticeship continues in other areas. She must learn a high level of mastery in the principles of sacred geometry, number symbolism, Native American philosophy, and creation mythology.

There comes a day, though, when she makes a leap of faith. The mental struggle and the emotional struggle cease. She moves through her inner turmoil into her sacred center. For the first time, she is able to sit down at her loom with no anger. She sits in total stillness. Then, like Spider Woman in the creation myth from the Native American tradition, she weaves together the cords of Heaven and Earth. From that still, sacred center, wherein lies the creative center of her being, comes the knowing to weave intricate, beautiful designs. She sits in the place of no thought, no concern about the past, no worry about the future. All she needs is given to her. She is both weaver and the one being woven. Only the moment. Only trust.

How long Jeremy gazed at the Sacred Mountain,
we can't be sure. For such moments exist in a space
somewhere beyond time.

CHAPTER THREE

Death of Trust

All of a sudden, everything changed. Instead of landing on familiar ground, the little mouse splashed down in water. And mice, as you know, can't swim very well. Jeremy was terrified. He flailed his legs about, trying to keep head above water, choking and sputtering, struggling for his very life. He was frightened nearly to death. Finally, he managed to make his way to the river bank.

"You tricked me. . .you tricked me!" Little Mouse yelled at the frog.

Feeling Betrayed

Jeremy felt betrayed! Betrayal is the death of trust. We feel betrayed when our expectations are not met, when someone or something we trusted turns out to be different than what we had hoped for or what we anticipated. We, in turn, lose trust in others and in our ability to know whom and what to trust. In the ultimate sense, however, no person or experience can ever betray us. There is nothing anyone can do that can ever change who we are or alter our worth as a person. Our worth is never dependent on anyone else's action or evaluation. Our value is simply not negotiable.

The lesson is not to stop trusting. Instead, it is to *always trust others and to trust who they are in reality,* rather than who or what we want them to be. We create images of who we think others are and are disappointed when the images are not real. The more we love and trust ourselves, the less need there is to project those parts of our ourselves we have disowned onto others.

Jeremy was furious with the frog! The frog was not who Jeremy wanted him to be, and his experience with the frog was not what he expected. Jeremy never thought he would land in water! The frog gave him no warning of what would happen once he took his leap. No need, really, to blame the frog, for the frog was simply being the frog! But Jeremy could not yet clearly see the frog, for he was just beginning to discover his own true identity.

Initiators as Tricksters

The role of the Frog in our lives is decidedly different from that of the Raccoon. The Raccoon is a guide, one who shows the way. The Frog, on the other hand, is an initiator, one who demands change. The concept of *initiator* is ancient in origin but is still relevant in our modern world.

In the past, certain cultures provided Mystery Schools for those students committed to the understanding of Universal Laws and the deeper mysteries of life. These schools, located in secluded settings in Greece, Egypt, Persia, India, Syria, China, and elsewhere, were opportunities for students to disengage from ordinary consensus reality and to focus instead on ancient spiritual truths. The teachings were revealed in the language of the Soul: through myth, metaphor, literature, music, art, and ritual.

These Mystery Schools provided the perfect opportunity for the student to study the microcosm in the macrocosm. They were places of special initiatory experiences in the sacred mysteries. Initiators crafted the specific initiation, or lesson, appropriate for each particular student. Initiations were opportunities to alter perception. Passing an initiation signaled the moving from one state of consciousness to another, the comprehension of the esoteric—inner—principle behind the exoteric—outer—form. It indicated that the student discerned the deeper meaning of an experience in his (or her) life. In practical terms, it meant that the next time that student was confronted with a similar situation, he would not be triggered; he would *respond* and not *react*.

Although we may never be in an official Mystery School or may never have a spiritual teacher as our initiator, we are, nonetheless, enrolled in the Mystery School called Life. And we most certainly have initiators in our lives, even though they bear no official title and may be totally unaware of how effective they are in their roles. Our initiators are those persons who challenge us, push our buttons, get in our way, participate in our dramas. Any mother-in-law, former husband, difficult child, cantankerous boss, or demanding friend will do! Initiators help to shape our characters. They show us our weaknesses and throw us back on ourselves. And they challenge us to sink beneath confusion to deeper levels of wisdom.

In the Mystery School of Life, we experience both minor and major initiations. Minor initiations are lessons in single areas of our lives, such as relationships or money or self-worth, etc. (There can be an infinite number and variety of these minor initiations.) Major initiations occur usually once, sometimes twice, in a lifetime. They are across-the-board experiences, signaled, on the outer level, by simultaneous changes in almost every aspect of our lives, which can include changes in self-identity, location, career, relationship, money matters, friends, interests, goals, etc. A major initiation, such as the one Jeremy must confront, requires a major shift in identity from the Ego Self to the Soul Self.

The task of the initiator is to break down all the former notions of "self." Initiators take us beyond the limitations of ego to the Soul, that part of us which has always been connected to the eternal. Jeremy, on his own, would never have made the leap of faith. It is only by the tricking of the frog that Jeremy was willing to go beyond his limited ego self. And even when he did jump, seeing something beyond the parameters of what he had always known almost caused him to drown.

Initiators perform their tasks in a variety of ways. The frog, in our story, played the role of trickster. Tricksters are shape-shifters. They wear disguises; they deceive. One never knows when they will pop up or what forms they will take. In the East, there are many stories of gurus who purposely disguise themselves as beggars to test the limits of their unsuspecting students and see how they will treat a nameless beggar on the street. These gurus shape-shift, or trick, their *chelas,* their students, in order to push them beyond their ego boundaries into the deeper mysteries of life. The ego, the structure we build to give us our self-identity, knows there is something else beyond itself but is hesitant to let go. The ego wants to be immortal, to be safe from all suffering, to be successful, prosperous, and loved. Above all, the ego wants the world to make sense in a way that the rational mind can comprehend.

Although tricksters can appear at any time and in any form, they seem to appear especially at those times when the ego becomes over-identified with the Innocent or the Orphan archetype. At this point in the story, Jeremy was very much an Innocent. Carol Pearson describes this archetype as wanting "to deny

unpleasant truth and just have faith and follow blindly." The frog awakens the little mouse, the Innocent,
to depth and discernment, to paradoxes, and to the
wholeness of life.

Most of us do not consciously choose a major
initiation. It seeks us out. Jeremy saw the Sacred
Mountain because he was tricked, or shocked, into
that sacred space. We may be shocked or disoriented
through any number of ways: physical pain, sudden
loss, a paranormal occurrence, a vivid dream, an
out-of-body experience, an experience with other
dimensions, etc. The ego will struggle to figure the
experience out by analyzing and rationalizing and by
trying to control. But those strategies are not adequate
to understand life at a Soul level. Passing the initiation
has little to do with the amount of trauma or dis-
orientation we experience. Initiation has to do with
our willingness to be awakened by the experience.
We must be willing, even, to *not* understand immediately what an experience means, and to trust the
process, knowing that in time the learning will come.

And in time, insights would come to Jeremy, and
he would continue his journey a much more seasoned
traveler.

Confronting Paradox

Again, Jeremy shouted, "You tricked me!"

*Undisturbed by Jeremy's screaming, the frog said
calmly, "Wait. No harm came to you. You saw the
Sacred Mountain, didn't you? Let go of your anger
and fear. It can blind you. What matters is what
happened. What did you see?"*

*The little mouse, still shivering from the fear or
landing in the water, could hardly speak. He stammered, "The. . .the Sacred Mountain!"*

"You are no longer just a little mouse. You have a new name. You are Jumping Mouse."
"Oh, thank you," said a startled Jumping Mouse. "Thank you, thank you."

On the one hand, the frog was the one who encouraged him to take the leap which allowed him to see the Sacred Mountain. On the other hand, the frog tricked him. He landed in water! Is the frog trustworthy or is he deceptive? Who is the real frog? Divine paradox at its best!

In the Mystery tradition, the student was challenged repeatedly with paradox and required to resolve it. The resolution of the paradox is never in choosing either extreme. It is not that the frog is either deceptive or trustworthy. Either/or thinking does not bring resolution. Nor does resolution come in denial or suppression of feelings in pretending, for example, that there is no anger. Neither is there resolution in compromise, in some lukewarm midway point between the two extremes. Nor can there be resolution in trying to transcend the paradox and questing for that state of bliss beyond all experience. Certainly, we are able to transcend this third-dimensional reality, but transcendence is at a later stage in the journey, not at the beginning.

The only way out of the paradox is through it. We must accept and embrace the opposites, deal with the pain and open to the joy. On the one hand, Jumping Mouse was tricked. From another perspective, the experience was a gift. The frog was both deceptive and trustworthy. Once we accept the opposites, we can see the whole of which paradoxes are the two opposite ends. We accept light/dark, right/wrong, joy/pain, sickness/health, rich/poor, being/non-being. To embrace paradox is to learn about death, dissolution, dismemberment, sex, passion, and ecstasy, and to see the beauty in it all. To embrace paradox is to see the divine interplay between life and death, confusion and harmony, matter and spirit. It is to come to terms with the conflicting forces in nature within ourselves and within others. In the end, it is to acknowledge the divinity within paradox, to open our hearts and embrace it all.

Before he gives Jeremy his new name, the frog says, "Let go of your anger and fear." Emotions must be owned and dealt with. The challenge is to deal with them and not get stuck in them. Letting go of disturbing emotions is often a very delicate and painful process. A Zen story illustrates the point.

> Once a Zen Master and his disciple were making a long journey. When they approached a stream, there was a young woman standing there, bewildered. She could not cross on her own and did not know what to do. Without any hesitation, the Master bowed to her respectfully, picked her up in his arms, and carried her across the stream. He put her down on the other side, bowed once again, and continued on his way.
>
> Nothing was said about the experience. By the time night came, the disciple could stand it no longer. He broke the silence of the journey. "Master," he said, "I have something I must say to you."
>
> "Speak," the Master replied.
>
> "You are a Zen Master," the disciple observed. "It is not permitted for you to carry a woman in your arms."
>
> "My son," the Master replied, "I put her down on the other side of the stream, many hours ago, but you are still carrying her in your heart."

The disciple was being challenged to move through paradox and *let go*. . .and Jumping Mouse was asked to move through paradox and *let go*.

Once there was a Frog who I was convinced had betrayed me. Through him, I had definitely seen the Mountain, but I had also spent a great deal of time flailing around in the water. In retrospect, it is clear that the Frog was a perfect mirror for where I was, a reflection of what was inside me. Again, it was just a Frog being a Frog! For several years I had carried anger about this Frog, feeling quite justified about my position. But no matter how much self-justification I felt, I was the one still stuck. Like Jeremy, I was blinded by anger and fear. It was time to *let go.*

I went to a Native American Sweat Lodge Ceremony, an ancient purification ritual for healing. I entered the lodge, a small dome-shaped structure, and took my place with others around the circle and sat cross-legged on the ground. In the center was an open pit with a glowing fire of hot, volcanic rocks. The Sweat Lodge is paradoxical in its very nature. There is hot and cold, light and dark, pain and joy. If one can embrace the opposites, a greater truth enters. I sat silently for a long while in the inky darkness of the lodge and waited for clarity. I began to understand my paradox: first exalting this man who had played the role of Frog, and later discounting him. He had been both deceptive and trustworthy, a mirror for the duality within me. The more important question was: had I seen the Sacred Mountain?

When it was my turn to pray to the grandfathers of the North, South, East, and West, I asked for healing. I was told to do a ceremony: to take a clay pot and to hold it five feet above a rock and then drop it. Shattering the pot would shatter the pattern.

I waited several weeks for an auspicious moment for the ceremony. Easter Sunday morning seemed the appropriate time. I carefully selected a particular clay pot, one given me many years before by a close friend. The small earthenware vase had been my friend's first effort as a potter; at the time, we both had considered it beautiful. Over the years, her work had matured, and that same pot now seemed awkward and unrefined; it had had its time and was now outmoded. The pot was a perfect metaphor for the occasion.

I walked five miles or so down the beach, watching the ocean tide rolling in and out, nodding at an occasional passerby. After an hour or so of walking, I reached the north end of the beach, the isolated sector of the oceanfront, silent and private. Immediately I was drawn to a rock of sizeable dimension, lying in the sand. It was as though it had been waiting for this moment to give itself to ceremony. With the clay pot in my right hand, I raised my arm high above my head. I called out to Great Spirit and dropped the pot onto the rock below, where it shattered into many pieces. Instantly, I was filled with amazing sounds—beautiful, full, rich tones and counter-tones, euphonious and melodious. The music was not of this world. I knew it to be the music of the spheres. I wanted to spread my arms wide and fly like an eagle.

Scenes from childhood flashed in my mind—the many times when I would go to the precipitous edge of a steep hillside, open my arms expansively and wait with hope for the time I could fly. On the beach, I was flying, except this time it didn't matter whether my body lifted off the ground. What mattered was that my spirit was soaring.

Resolving Paradox

The frog points Jumping Mouse beyond the paradox to the greater truth. "What did you see?" If we get stuck in either/or thinking, deciding that the frog is either trustworthy or deceptive, we stay stuck in duality. Whole truth contains opposites. If we can hold the opposites, and not get stuck in either the first or second condition, we allow room for the third condition, a higher truth, to reveal itself.

It is not insignificant that this *third* condition is such a vital step in our journey. In numerology the number three symbolizes unity, the trinity, the place of harmony. In the Native American Medicine Wheel the number three is also significant. The Medicine Wheel is a metaphor for the mind. There are corridors that lead out to the four directions, the East (the mental), the South (the emotional), the West (the physical), and the North (the spiritual). Inherent in the Medicine Wheel is a five-step process that Nature gives us to make decisions. (Sometimes the entire five-step process occurs in a split second. Other times, we get stuck for months, or even years, at some place within the Medicine Wheel.) The East—the mental—is first on the wheel. It is the direction where there is unity in all things, where wisdom enters. In the direction of the South—the emotional, the second step—we deal with duality, with paradoxes. The direction of the West—the physical, step three—is the place of reconciliation of the opposites. Then we go to the North, the spiritual, to find direction and purpose and finally to the Center, which completes the circle and is the place of transformational possibilities.

It was the third step—the West—that Jeremy encountered at the moment the frog answered the accusation that he had betrayed Jeremy.

"Let go of your anger and fear. . .What did you see?" asked the frog. What did you learn from the experience? Focus on new wisdom, not old pain. Move through duality. How were you changed? In what way have you been enriched or deepened by the experience? Are you more compassionate, more genuine, more aware, more feeling? Don't waste the experience. Let it serve you.

Jeremy saw the Sacred Mountain and in so doing gained a new name. In the beginning of the story, he lived as Jeremy in Mouse Village, on the periphery of the Self. Next, he progressed to the River, which was closer to who he was. But when he saw the Mountain, metaphorically he saw the Heart of God. He caught a glimpse of his real self and his own sacred dimension.

"You have a new name," said the frog. "You are Jumping Mouse." When what we learn from any painful experience, whether it be an initiatory experience, a re-birth, a betrayal experience, or simply a difficult time, is greater than the amount of pain we have invested in it, we know that we have successfully moved through and beyond the experience. The new name is the indication that Jumping Mouse has indeed passed his initiation.

In the ancient traditions, initiations were often accompanied by physical trauma, such as physical scarring or having the Medicine Man knock out a tooth. Such shocks were the outer manifestation of an inner change. Jeremy is plunged into water. Emersion in water is associated with baptismal rites, the symbolic death to the old life and the birth of the new. As soon as the little mouse is immersed in water, the frog immediately gives Jeremy his new name, Jumping Mouse. New names often are an integral part of ceremonies and rites of passage. The new name carries with it a new vibration, a new identity, a new sense of self. Jesus re-named his disciples; gurus give spiritual names to their devotees; and Catholic nuns are given new names when they take their vows. And naming is often an integral part of both confirmation and baptismal ceremonies. The name Jumping Mouse is a reminder to the little mouse of a new identity. His former self has been transformed into a newborn being. He is no longer a little mouse limited to hurrying and scurrying with his whiskers in the ground. He is *Jumping* Mouse. He will see all of life from a much different perspective.

The Inflation Stage

Jumping Mouse stood up and shook off the water. And he shook off the anger and fear. He thought instead about the beauty of the Sacred Mountain.

He thought, "I must go back and tell my people what has happened." He couldn't wait to share. Surely, they would be eager to hear his stories of the river and the mountain.

With great excitement, Jumping Mouse set off for Mouse Village. Everyone would be so pleased to see him. And surely they would be interested in his story. Why, there might even be a celebration in his honor!

Most of us have had the experience of having a transformative experience and wanting to share it, immediately, with others, whether or not they want to hear it and whether or not it is appropriate to share! Jumping Mouse fantasized a triumphant return to Mouse Village. It would be obvious that he had had a unique experience because he was still wet from the river. Everyone would be curious about what happened to him and would insist he tell them his story. No doubt they would sit spell-bound in amazement. They might even have a party, or a celebration, just for him!

Carl Jung warns about getting over-identified with the transcendent realm. Jumping Mouse had had a glimpse of the Mountain. For a moment, at least, he had seen the other side. When the ego becomes inflated, it assumes and absorbs the manna of the transcendent realm as if it were a part of itself. This inability to differentiate *other* from *self* is called the Inflation Stage. In this state, we are similar to the infant who cannot differentiate himself from others; the ego assumes the mountain is part of itself, too. In this stage, we are attached to the result of our action. It matters what others think. We must have impact. We have to impress. We want to be noticed, to be special, to be separate.

Jumping Mouse was still new to the journey. In time, he would gain spiritual maturity and learn discernment. Some spiritual experiences are best not shared or at least not shared for some time. They need a period of incubation. We need to hold them a while in our hearts. With maturity, we eventually realize that our experiences are both highly personal and very impersonal. We don't need to be "separate" from others in order to experience sacred moments. Our experiences are unique to us and available to everyone.

> *When Jumping Mouse arrived, he was still wet. But it hadn't rained in Mouse Village and everyone else was dry! There was great discussion as to why Jumping Mouse was wet. Could it be that he had been swallowed by some horrible beast and then spit out again? That would mean there was something horribly wrong with this mouse. Fear took hold; who knew what could happen once you left Mouse Village?*
>
> *No one wanted to spend time with Jumping Mouse. His stories about the river and the Sacred Mountain fell on deaf ears.*

Jumping Mouse was crushed. We love to be valued, to be acknowledged, to be able to share who we are and what we experience and to have our identity and our experiences validated. But the real test comes when the outer world, or those persons whose responses we value, cannot or do not understand our truth. Do we give up our reality? Do we change it slightly so it can be acceptable? Do we become bitter and critical of the inadequacies of others? Do we insist on convincing others of our actuality in some desperate effort to win their favor and in so doing regain their acceptance?

Trusting Your Own Truth

Some years ago, a group gathered for a "forty days in the wilderness" experience. It was a program designed for deep inner work. Midway through the program, a young woman named Anna experienced what she considered to be a profound visionary experience. During group time, she began to describe her revelation in vivid detail. Her friends sat listening intently to the story, enthralled with her every word, inspired with the hope that they might one day have a similar experience. Everyone was captivated—everyone, that is, except an East Indian teacher who sat crossed-legged in the back of the room with his gaze focused downward. When she finished sharing her vision, he spoke in a sharp tone. "Your story, though interesting, is far from being a true visionary experience. It is pure projection and fantasy. Such experiences are born out of ego, and the ego dies hard."

There was a hush in the room. Everything changed. Suddenly, no one was interested in her experience. Her former friends suddenly were suspicious. No one believed her anymore. She felt betrayed, but she never gave up her truth. . .her belief that hers was truly a visionary experience. In her heart, Anna knew what is so well expressed in *A Course in Miracles*: "Nothing real can be threatened; nothing unreal exists."

We usually look to those closest to us for our validation. Because they matter the most, these are the ones who hurt us the most. If we depend on validation of self from others, invariably there comes a time when outside approval is withdrawn. Such experiences ultimately help us become aware of our need for healing. We are faced with our own shadows. We must confront our deepest fears. We are required to test the depth of our trust in our own truth.

Months later, that same East Indian said to Anna, "I always knew you had a true visionary experience, but I didn't know if you had the courage to trust your own truth."

> *Even though no one in Mouse Village believed Jumping Mouse, in time it didn't matter. He never forgot his vision of the Sacred Mountain. Jumping Mouse stayed in Mouse Village, but of course now life was different. But then, he was different.*

The familiar Buddhist story says it well:

> "What did you do before you became enlightened?"
> "I chopped wood, and I carried water."
> "What did you do after you became enlightened?"
> "I chopped wood, and I carried water."

CHAPTER FOUR

Facing Doubt

*J*umping Mouse settled quietly into life in Mouse Village. For a while, that is. But there came a day when he knew he must leave. The memory of the Sacred Mountain was not one he could forget. He knew that somehow he must find his way there.

Once again, Jumping Mouse went to the edge of Mouse Village and looked out onto the prairie. This time, there was no raccoon waiting. There was no path, even. He knew that now he must find his own way. He looked up in the sky for eagles. It was full of many brown spots, each one an eagle. At any moment, they could swoop down from the sky. Even though his heart was pounding with fear, Jumping Mouse was determined to go to the Sacred Mountain. And so, gathering all his courage, he ran just as fast as he could onto the prairie.

Trusting the Unmarked Path

When Jumping Mouse first left Mouse Village, he was motivated more by curiosity than by conviction. He relied on the knowledge of the raccoon, a seasoned guide, to lead him to his discoveries. In the beginning of our journey too, we may need to follow the footsteps of another in order to find our way. Reliance on others is both acceptable and expected. But as the journey continues, we must make the transition from depending on others for direction to trusting within ourselves. We must find our own way on the unmarked path.

This time, when Jumping Mouse left Mouse Village, no raccoon was waiting. Jumping Mouse had to search out his own truth. Curiosity had to give way to conviction; doubt had to yield to inner certainty.

At this stage of our journey, we may be hesitant to proceed on our own. We may decide to wait for yet another Raccoon to lead us to the River. . .or remain on the banks of the River transfixed by the roar of the River. . .or retreat to the life we once knew in Mouse Village. Once we return to the status quo of Mouse Village, we can discount the significance of the River. We can convince ourselves that we never saw the Mountain. Or we can minimize the impact of the experience by reducing it to a minor incident. We can choose from a plethora of options. And we are free to stop at any point along the path.

If we want to continue on our journey, we must be willing to proceed without a Raccoon. For if we insist on depending on outside help when it is not needed, we may face dramatic consequences. The very sources which once proved reliable may suddenly become erratic and give misinformation, perhaps quite unintentionally. Or perhaps the sources we seek simply cannot, or are not, willing to assist. It is as though there is a conspiracy of a higher order which insists we pass this initiation of confronting doubt so we can move to a deeper level of inner trust.

A young American whom we will call Gordon traveled all the way to France, hoping to receive guidance from a Raccoon of his own choosing, a revered teacher. As so often happens, guidance was given, but it was far different from what Gordon had expected.

Gordon, who had been a student of ancient wisdom for a number of years, had been, during the course of his studies, particularly impressed with the works of Frederic Lionel, a Frenchman who authored a number of books on esoteric subjects. The trip to France was, in a sense, a spiritual pilgrimage; Gordon was at a critical juncture in his life. He had reached an impasse. Even though he had sensed his Sacred Call during a much earlier period, had made his way to the River, and had even glimpsed the Sacred Mountain, now he was suddenly doubting. He was indecisive. He did not know where to turn or how to take the next step.

Gordon decided to enlist the help of Frederic Lionel. If that meant a trip to France, so be it! He was determined to seek out sage words of advice from a man he considered a spiritual giant. After a series of letters and phone calls to France, an appointment was arranged. As a way of introducing himself, Gordon forwarded copies of several readings which had been given for him by well-known psychics.

At the arranged time several months later, Gordon knocked on the door of a charming Parisian flat. He was greeted cordially by Frederic Lionel's wife and then ushered into a room and seated at a small wooden table across from Frederic. In his eighties, Frederic had an imposing presence which spoke of aristocracy and nobility. He was tall and regal, and a shock of thick white hair framed his finely chiseled features. His eyes riveted Gordon with a quick glance that shot through him all the way down to his toes. Frederic made no effort to engage in small talk or social pleasantries. Instead, there was a deafening silence. Gordon inadvertently began to compare himself with the commanding presence of this legendary man and found himself lacking in the comparison. Both men sat silently, pensively, as moments extended into some indeterminable length of time. Then, with great precision, Frederic clasped his hands together, as though to gesture the coming together of thoughts. Slowly, ceremoniously, he placed his hands on the table and proceeded to look into Gordon's eyes with a penetrating gaze. His questions were equally piercing.

"Why are you here?" he asked.

Gordon gave a carefully measured response. "I want to get in touch with a voice inside that is truth, one that I can always hear."

"What are you afraid of?" responded Frederic. "Young man, do you know that your insistence on seeking outside sources has gotten you nowhere?"

He then referenced the readings which Gordon had sent ahead. "Yes, I read them. Your reliance on others has imprisoned you. Get rid of your atavism, your need to put others on a pedestal. I don't even want you to believe what I am saying. Go inside yourself. What makes you think others have better access than you do? You are looking everywhere except right where you are. How can you advance spiritually if you don't dare to become a free state of being?"

Gordon quickly responded, "I see. What you are saying is that I need to be in the center of my circle."

"No" was the answer. "You are not understanding what I am saying at all. You *are* the center of your circle. Take this project that you are beginning. It is good to have a final vision. But you make a mistake in letting the vision get in the way. You must start to let the flower unfold, without picking at the bud. Become quiet each morning. Listen to your intuition and follow what it says *now*. It may only be a small thing, like writing a letter or making a call. The important thing is that you trust what comes. Listen to what you feel. Trust it totally, and do it right away. If no response comes, it means you are not supposed to receive anything. It means your phone is busy. At those times, even if you were to listen, you could not hear. Your ego would argue and get in the way, somehow. The river is always in progress. Be in the river. It is all up to you. Do you have any more questions?"

Gordon was quiet for a moment and then said, "Nothing more."

"Good," said Frederic. "Then maybe you have understood something of what I have told you."

Gordon fell silent as he sat looking at a man who knew unequivocally that of which he spoke. Frederic's knowledge of esoteric wisdom had been fully tested in the arena of life. Gordon had heard numerous accounts of his heroic deeds during World War II, when Frederic was a recognized leader of the French underground resistance. For four years, he had managed to stay ahead of the Nazis by doing precisely what he now passed on to Gordon: Listen within—to hunches, feelings, visceral responses, intuitive flashes, and inner knowings, and trust the response.

Certainly, any lingering tendency Gordon had to continue waiting for a Raccoon had been dispelled. He had his answer—not the one he had come to hear, but the one that was needed to continue his journey.

Listening Within

With no Raccoon to guide, we, like Gordon and Jumping Mouse, must learn to listen within. How is it that most people go through enormous struggles to acquire inner trust while others seemingly have a natural propensity to trust, instead of doubting, their inner voice?

Perhaps there is no easy answer to that question, no formula or identifiable cluster of characteristics which can clearly designate what ensures inner trust. But I have noticed a striking commonality in those persons who have a natural ability to listen within. As children, they listened to and trusted outer authority which was trustworthy—outer authority which deserved their trust. As adults, they were able to shift gracefully from listening to outer authority to listening to inner authority. Children who trust false or unreliable authority, however, find it more difficult to make that graceful shift in adulthood. Consider German youth who, during World War II, listened obediently to the existing authority, or children of abusive parents who listen to also-untrustworthy authority. As adults, these children have a much more challenging task of learning to discern what is trustworthy in both their outer worlds and their inner worlds.

My father is an example of a person who had a natural ability to listen within. He not only was gifted intuitively but also had an amazing power of discernment. As a child, I observed time and time again as he would look at a person or a situation and just *know*. He had a profound, natural wisdom. No hesitation. No confusion. No vacillation. Just *knowing*.

I loved listening to his heartwarming stories about growing up in the foothills of the Blue Ridge Mountains. The tales, told in a charming Waltonesque style, reflected a love of the land and portrayed the delightful and amusing antics of his brothers and sisters. Somehow, though, I took lightly his insistence that he had always been obedient to his father. Perhaps it was the choice of the word *obedient*, which felt terribly old-fashioned and uncomfortable to young sensitive ears. But at family get-togethers, when childhood anecdotes were often retold in this family of gifted storytellers, his brothers and sisters would invariably affirm that indeed Guy, my dad, was the most obedient child. He had always listened and had done what he was told "right away."

The correlation between my father's obedience and his trust in his inner self escaped me until years later when I had a conversation with Joseph Rael, who has an indisputable link to Spirit. I was struck by the realization that this theme ran through the childhoods of both men. While Joseph and I co-authored *Being and Vibration*, we would talk about the events in his childhood. In our discussions it became clear that an essential part of his early training was to "pay attention" and "listen" to how all of life was speaking to him. Paying attention included obedience to the elders. Joseph listened well. His response to authority was always the same: immediate and consistent. That capacity to listen would prove to be critical later.

In 1984, Joseph asked Spirit for a vision which might show him how best to serve the earth and honor all life. The vision came in a flash of light. In linear time, it may have lasted only two or three minutes, but in the place where visions appear, time, as we know it, does not exist. In this vision, Joseph was told to build Sound Chambers around the world. These chambers would be places where people whose spirits and voices resonate in absolute harmony would come to balance the present, the future, and the memory of how the cosmos is oriented through the use of sound.

I was curious as to why it was he, not someone else, who was chosen to receive the vision for the Sound Chambers. Joseph says, with a glint in his eye, that he asked the grandfathers on the other side that same question. "Was it because I am talented? Because I am deserving? Because I am worthy?"

The answer was surprising and disarming. "It isn't any of these reasons. It is because you listen. We knew you would do what you were told."

Resisting Country Mouse Comfort

Jumping Mouse ran until he came to a mound of sage. He was safe now, out of view of those brown spots in the sky. He was resting and trying to catch his breath when he saw a kind old mouse, a country gentleman. This patch of sage, which was home for the old mouse, was a haven indeed. There were plentiful seeds, varieties which he had never seen, and material for making nests. So many things for a mouse to be busy with.

"Hello," said the kindly old mouse. "Welcome to my home."

Jumping Mouse was amazed. He had never seen such a place. Or such a mouse! "What a wonderful place you have. You have everything here. And you are even safe from the eagles. I have never seen such a place like this before."

"Yes," smiled the kindly old mouse, "it is safe here. And from here, you can see all the beings of the prairie. Why, there are buffalo and rabbit and coyote and fox and. . ."

Jumping Mouse listened in amazement as the old mouse named every animal of the prairie. Why, he knew all their names by heart!

"Sir, what about the river and the mountains? Can you also see them?"

"Well, little friend, you can certainly see the river. I know of the river. But as to the mountain, I am afraid that does not exist. It is just a myth, a story that people enjoy telling. Young man, take my advice and forget about the mountain. Everything you could want is here. You can stay with me for as long as you like. And besides, this is the best place to be."

For a moment, Jumping Mouse questioned his decision to go to the Sacred Mountain. He was tempted to stay put and make a life here with Country Mouse. This was such a comfortable place. And cer-

tainly it was far greater than the life he had known in Mouse Village.

There is a temptation, once we leave Mouse Village and discover Country Mouse, to become satisfied with our initial breakthrough. We decide we have found *It*. We know we have grown beyond where we were. We rationalize that we don't really need to take more risks or strive to extend our inner or outer limits. *It* is comfortable and *It* is safe. We stop growing. We become stuck in form. We settle for a mental system and forgo the heart journey.

There was a time when I, like Jumping Mouse, had to decide whether to stay with Country Mouse or leave. I was deeply involved with a spiritual organization, and, for the most part, my association with the group had been a fruitful one. But I had reached the inevitable crossroad. Change was imminent, but I conveniently avoided a decision about my future by staying in doubt and confusion. Deep down, I knew there were only two choices. Either I must make a clean break and leave the organization altogether, or I could stay. But if I stayed, it must be in a decidedly different capacity. It wasn't an easy decision. For one thing, there was a strong emotional pull from other group members, people with whom I had bonded by sharing important steps in our mutual journey. They seemed satisfied to be Country Mice and were quite convincing as they sought to encourage me, as well as others, to stay put. Country Mice want others to stay where they are. Their insistence stems both from their genuine satisfaction in the existing form and, partly, from their own fear of moving beyond the familiar.

I had to reconcile the murmurings of my heart, which were calling me to other horizons, with the loyalty I felt toward this organization, which had become my Country Mouse. The concepts learned in this organization, which had once freed me from the limitations of Mouse Village, I now found limiting.

I had vacillated long enough. It was time to make a decision. Early one morning, from that still place deep inside, I asked Spirit to give me a clear answer within twenty-four hours, one that could not possibly be missed. This ancient form of prayer, called *precipitation,* is based on the universal law which says that we create (precipitate), or draw to us, anything that our consciousness is capable of believing we deserve. The process of precipitation involves first "putting out a thought in Spirit," then letting go of all anxiety surrounding that thought, and, finally, letting go of any expectations as to the specific way the request will be answered. In this way, a void is created for something new to enter—a new thought, a new insight, a sign or a symbol.

That evening, I went to a restaurant with a group of fifteen or so people who were members of the organization. We were in a rather jovial mood, laughing and talking with an ease born out of long-term friendship and mutual experience. Halfway through the meal, something became lodged in my throat. I was choking. I could not swallow. I could not breathe. It happened so quickly that no one even noticed.

Suddenly, I was aware of two realities at once. The Physical-I was choking; the Observer-I was in another reality, witnessing the scene from above with absolute calm.

Eventually, the person sitting on my right noticed that something was wrong and began to gently pat my back. The Observer-I thought, "That is nice, but a pat on the back is not going to do it!" I tried to take a sip of water. There was no relief. I bent over in an effort to dislodge whatever it was that was stuck. That didn't work, either.

The Observer-Self was curious about the physical phenomenon of oxygen deprivation. I wondered how long a person could live without air. Did a person turn blue, pass out? Exactly what was the sequential order? Maybe it had been a long time already. Somehow, from that observer space, linear time had little relevance and certainly there was no anxiety about anything. The seriousness of the situation somehow eluded the Observer-Self. In fact, it all seemed rather amusing. Here was a table full of healers, and not one of them knew how to handle this emergency!

The Observer-Self suggested I stand up. Immediately, the waiter, who happened to be a friend, sensed my difficulty. He rushed over to where I was and said, "Mary Elizabeth, you can't breathe, can you?"

I shook my head no.

Without wasting a second, he skillfully placed his hands around me in the position of the well-known Heimlich maneuver. With a quick jerk, he lifted me off the ground and dislodged the piece of food from my throat. All of a sudden, I could breathe again! I took several long, deep breaths. The oxygen was welcomed by every cell of my body. It wasn't until sometime later that I discovered my waiter friend had learned the Heimlich technique only the night before!

I had my answer. No more doubt. Spirit had responded in no uncertain terms! I was choking in this organization. My throat, the fifth chakra, the will center, the metaphor for self-expression, was being shut off. It was time for me to be on my own and make my way to the Sacred Mountain.

It is never easy to leave Country Mouse, especially when he tells us that the Sacred Mountain is only a myth! If we listen to our hearts, however, we can hear the message and know when and if it is time to leave. It is seldom that the message is given in such dramatic form as a literal choking! But if we listen, we can hear the message nonetheless.

Facing Doubt

Jumping Mouse listened carefully to the words of Country Mouse, especially what he had to say about the Sacred Mountain.

"How can you say that the Great Mountain is only a myth?" challenged Jumping Mouse. "Once I saw the Sacred Mountain, and it is not something one can ever forget."

Jumping Mouse had his own answer. He knew he must go. He thanked Country Mouse for making him feel so welcome and for sharing his home. "I cannot stay longer. I must go now, to seek the Mountain."

"You are a foolish mouse, indeed, if you leave here. The prairie is a dangerous place, especially for a little mouse! Why, just look up in the sky. The old mouse pointed dramatically to the sky. See up there? Those spots are eagles, just waiting for a little mouse. They can see for miles. And they will catch you!"

The fear that those brown spots would swoop down was actually a much greater fear of Country Mouse projected onto Jumping Mouse. What if Great Spirit were to swoop down out of the sky and take Country Mouse out of his limited ego self? What if those eagles were to lift him up to see from another perspective?

No doubt, Country Mouse had already risked once, when he left Mouse Village years ago. Now he is comfortably situated in a lifestyle and a philosophical system which works. He has gone far beyond what he knew in Mouse Village. . .You mean there might be more?

To confront Country Mouse is to confront that part of ourselves that doubts our journey to the

Sacred Mountain. How committed are we to following that which, to us, is sacred? What is it that we will not compromise? What are we willing to risk? Once we are certain about our path, the doubts and fears of Country Mouse will not matter. What we hold sacred will determine all else in our lives.

The I Ching, the Oriental book of changes, contains ancient philosophical wisdom. The book is composed of sixty-four hexagrams in which the Oracle counsels about action and attitudes that are appropriate in the midst of outer change. *The I Ching* emphasizes holding to inner values and living in harmony with the Tao in the middle of a continually changing universe.

According to the teachings, when heaven and earth come together, they give birth to the first son. The first son's name is Intuition. Intuition is the flash of inspiration, a certainty which defies the rational mind, a feeling that persists, a deep sense of inner knowing.

As soon as we give birth to our first son, Intuition, another son follows on his heels. This second son's name is Doubt, the linear, rational, reasoning mind. He tests our trust in our own truth. Doubt is the questioning thoughts which cause us to second-guess our original knowing. He is the chattering voice of our Monkey Mind that discounts and denies. And Doubt is the critical and skeptical voices of the people in our outer world who serve as mirrors to reflect our inner confusion.

Doubt comes again and again to challenge our certainty about ourselves and our choices. When we doubt, we settle. We settle for our fears, and we settle for the fears of others. We settle for beliefs which limit. We settle for the truth of others. We settle for less than what we are, for less than what could be. We settle. . .rather than trusting our innermost feelings.

Resolving Doubt

The I Ching tells us how to resolve doubt. Once the second son Doubt (the rational mind) is born, we must go to the High Mountain (Higher Mind). It is then that the third son, Stillness, is born. In this place we discover direct knowing.

Marie was a single woman in her late thirties in Norway who was faced with a critical choice. A highly educated professional woman, she became pregnant with a much-wanted child. Because of her age, which placed her in a high-risk pregnancy category, she was required to undergo amniocentesis.

She was stunned to learn that her unborn child carried Down's Syndrome! Her certainty about motherhood was suddenly replaced with doubt. Her doctor immediately tried to comfort her, saying, "I know this news is very hard to hear. As your doctor, it is my duty to give you my best advice. I would strongly encourage you to consider abortion as a viable option. All of my patients who have been faced with a similar situation have opted for abortion. Raising a child with Down's Syndrome is extremely difficult, especially for a single woman. You will have years of untold medical and emotional challenges facing you. And besides, you already have two healthy children. You are an attractive, intelligent and highly educated woman with your life ahead. Think of yourself." And then as a final note, he added, "Because of the rather advanced stage of your pregnancy, you have only a week to decide whether you want to terminate."

One week. Just seven days. Within that short span of time, she must make one of the most important decisions of her life! The easier course would probably be to take the very well-intentioned advice of her Country Mouse, her doctor. She would be quite justified with such a choice. Not only that, but the father of the child adamantly supported the doctor's position. It was painfully clear that a decision to keep the child would mean she, and she alone, would be the support of this child. A decision of this magnitude which involved the life of another could not be decided by logic alone. She wanted to listen to her deeper feelings, to the promptings of her heart.

Her High Mountain had always been the Dream World. Before going to bed that evening, she asked Great Spirit to come to her in a dream and grant her the wisdom to know with certainty what she should do. During the night, she had a very telling dream. In the dream, she saw her unborn son, a perfectly formed infant, but clearly a Mongoloid child. The dream dissipated any lingering hope that somehow a mistake had been made in the testing. But there was no mistake, either, in the tremendous love she felt for her unborn son. St. John of the Cross says, "Feelings are the language of God to the Soul." Theirs was a soul connection. No doubt now. This was indeed her child. Her son. The choice was no longer difficult. The next morning she announced her decision to her disbelieving doctor, her Country Mouse.

Trusting the Promptings of the Heart

A man from Norway, Ailo Gaup, had Country Mice of a different variety to confront, one that many indigenous people around the world have had to face. Ailo was born in the far north of Norway during World War II. With the war came the burning of houses and the destruction of roads. Ailo, along with many other children, was taken to a hospital for safety in the fall of 1944. His parents returned to the tundra, and conditions prevented them from returning for a year. When his parents were finally able to come and ask for him, the nurse at the hospital refused to return him to them. The hospital belonged to the Sami mission, and their unofficial practice included, as Ailo describes it, "saving" some children to send them south and make good Christian Norwegians out of them. Ailo was separated from his birthright—his family, his culture, his language, and his land—and was sent to grow up as part of a farm family in southern Norway. As if uprooting a child were not enough, his new family brutalized and terrorized him. In a sense he was their slave, and until the age of nineteen he was so fearful of consequences that he was afraid to leave, despite the most deplorable circumstances.

All information about Ailo's original family and culture was withheld. He was made to feel worthless and was told that he would never be able to make a life of his own. When we are severely shamed, part of us knows that what we are told cannot be true, but there is a part of us that is afraid that it might be true.

Although his family discouraged education, Ailo's one solace was reading. It was his one escape from cruelty, his only safety from the "shadowland." In literature he could touch feelings of love. He held tight to the hope that if love can be written about in books, then maybe it can exist somewhere in life. He was determined to listen to and learn from the promptings of his heart.

But by the time Ailo was nineteen, life had become so unbearable for him that, after what was to be his last beating, he lay in the barn at the point of suicide with a knife to his own throat. Suddenly, a "spirit of light" flew in though the wall, telling him not to take his life. . .telling him about his path and his destiny. That experience with light took away his sadness, his worry, and his hurt. He knew then with certainty what he must do. Ailo put his necessary belongings on his bicycle and left in the dark, in spite of the "brown spots that might reach down from the sky."

Years went by, and in time Ailo established a successful journalism career. But something deep inside him stirred. He longed to search for his biological mother and to explore his native roots. He was willing to give up all that he had, if need be, in order to satisfy this deeper calling. It would mean leaving his job and sacrificing his position on the paper. His journalism mentor, his Country Mouse, warned Ailo not to leave the security of his position for the impending uncertainty.

In spite of the admonishments and fears about what might lie ahead, that the "brown spots in the sky might swoop down," Ailo honored his commitment to himself and left for the far north. . .with no guarantees. So began the long hours of piecing together bits of information and going through the inevitable letdowns when hopes are kindled and then die sudden deaths.

In time, the painstaking research and patience were finally rewarded. The auspicious moment came when a elderly woman clothed in skins and hides entered a designated shelter in an isolated part of the icy tundra, where Ailo had been patiently waiting. The two sat across from each other in a pregnant silence; it was the long-awaited moment. Their eyes met and searched for a certainty that defies logic. Even amid the tears, he could clearly see his face in hers. There was no question, now. This woman was his mother.

She began to smoke a pipe and speak in a strange tongue which he did not understand but which stirred mysterious chords of memory. It was both the end and the beginning of a search. Although his search for his mother had ended, he would begin a lifetime quest to search the wisdom of the Lapps, also known as Sami. The journey would awaken a part of him heretofore asleep. In time, he would become a well-known shaman, a healer, and the author of numerous books and plays related to his native culture.

Of course, he could have stayed with Country Mouse.

And Jumping Mouse could have stayed with Country Mouse. For we can stop any place we want along the way. But even the fears and the doubts of Country Mouse were not strong enough to dissuade Jumping Mouse from following his own intuitive heart.

Even though Jumping Mouse listened as Country Mouse gave his fearful warnings, and even though in the sky there were still those brown spots. . .Jumping Mouse knew he must make his way to the Sacred Mountain. He stood still for a moment, took a deep breath, gathered his strength, and ran with all his might across the prairie.

CHAPTER FIVE

Opening the Intuitive Heart

*I*t was hard for Jumping Mouse to leave the comfortable life with Country Mouse. Out on the prairie was much to be afraid of. As Jumping Mouse gathered all his courage and ran as hard as he could, he could feel the brown spots flying high overhead. Would those brown spots really swoop down and catch him, just as Country Mouse had said? He shivered at the thought. He was truly in the unknown now.

All of a sudden, he ran into a stand of chokecherries. It was a wonderful place to explore. Why, there were things to gather, delicious seeds to eat, and many grasses for making nests. Jumping Mouse was busy investigating his new terrain when he saw an enormous, dark, furry thing lying motionless in the grass. He decided to climb up on it. There was a large mound to explore. There were even horns to climb on. That would be fun, thought Jumping Mouse. Immediately, he made his way on one of the horns, when all of a sudden he heard a sound. It sounded like a moan. It seemed to come from the dark furry thing! Quick as a wink, Jumping Mouse scurried down to the grass beneath. There was another moan, and the sound of deep breathing.

A voice said, "Hello, my brother."

"Who are you?" asked a curious Jumping Mouse.

"Why I am a buffalo!"

"A buffalo!" thought Jumping Mouse. Even in Mouse Village he had heard of the mighty buffalo!

Metaphor of the Buffalo

The buffalo appears at a time when it is difficult for Jumping Mouse to find his way on the unfamiliar terrain of the prairie. Mice are nearsighted. They tend to see only that which is close at hand. The old mouse way of seeing does not function well on the open prairie. If Jumping Mouse is to make his way through the challenges of this new landscape, he needs a broader perspective. He needs new inspiration. At the auspicious moment, Jumping Mouse meets Buffalo, the great giver of life.

Recently, I had the opportunity to observe a Buffalo Dance on a Pueblo reservation. The Buffalo Dance is a powerful ceremony which enacts the metaphor of how new ideas are planted in the psyche. For something new to enter, there must be an opening. We must first let go, either physically, mentally, emotionally, or spiritually. Either we willingly relinquish that which no longer serves us, or life creates situations which force us to let go. When we give up the ego, we create space for new thoughts to enter, for seeds to be planted in the psyche.

The Buffalo Dance begins when the dancers, males ranging in age from young to old, representing aspects of the masculine energy, climb out from the underground kiva. They dance first on an open space on one level and then move to a lower level, bringing to life the spiritual principle which says "As above, so below." As there is movement, or dance, which is the expansion of light in the upper world, that same movement is then brought into and expressed in the world of matter. Two men, representing the two worlds of spirit and matter, are dressed as buffalo. Their bodies are covered in buffalo skins and their heads are covered in magnificent buffalo headdresses. In their hands are long poles which they periodically poke in the earth, which is the metaphor for the self. As they poke their sticks in the earth, they symbolically plant new ideas in the earth/self. When there is an opening, or hole, in our psyche, we can receive insights from the higher dimensions. The dance dramatizes how ideas from the up-above world, or spiritual dimension, enter into the material realm.

While the buffalo poke holes in the earth, simultaneously another metaphor is being danced. At various intervals, some of the dancers, usually the younger boys, playfully run up to the buffalo, poke sticks at them, and then scurry away. The dancers want the buffalo to notice them. They want something from Spirit. They want new ideas, new inspiration, new thought. The old way of seeing life is no longer working. It has served its time. It is limited and outmoded. As soon as the dancers poke the buffalo, the buffalo, in turn, pursue and playfully poke the dancers. In a sense, the buffalo are saying, "You want something from us, but for you to receive anything, you must be open. You are blocked. You are closed off. Your ego is so strong that we will need to take our poles and poke holes in your psyche so you can give up your limited beliefs and perceptions. Once you let go of the ego, there is space. New insights can enter. We can give you new life. We can plant new ideas in your psyche."

Giving Up an Eye

Jumping Mouse had never before seen a buffalo. Certainly, no buffalo had ever lived in Mouse Village.

"What a magnificent being you are," Jumping Mouse said to Buffalo.

"Thank you, my little brother, for visiting me."

*"You are lying down. What is wrong?" asked the
little mouse."*

*"I am sick and I am dying," said Buffalo. "There is
only one thing that can save me. That is the eye of a
mouse. But there is no such thing as a mouse out here
on the prairie!"*

*The eye of a mouse! Jumping Mouse was
astonished! "You mean my tiny little eye could save
this magnificent being?" He darted back to the
chokecherries. He scurried back and forth. What to
do, what to do. But he could hear the breathing of the
buffalo. It was slowing down and becoming heavy.*

*"He will die," thought Jumping Mouse, "if I do not
give him my eye. He is such a magnificent being. I
cannot let him die."*

Jumping Mouse knew that the only way to save
the buffalo was to give up one of his tiny eyes. The
only way to save the buffalo, who represents a higher,
more inspired aspect himself, is to give up his mouse
way of seeing. Yogis go to the Himalayas; shaman
go to the desert; others enter the stillness in countless
other ways. They go that they might give up limited
sight and see instead with spiritual sight. Something
is required; something is given.

*With no time to waste, Jumping Mouse scurried back
to the spot where Buffalo lay. "I am a mouse," he said
with a shaky voice. "And you are such a magnificent
being. I cannot let you die. I have two eyes. If my eye can
save you, I will gladly give it to you."*

*The minute he spoke, Jumping Mouse's eye flew
out of his head and Buffalo was made whole. The
buffalo jumped to his feet, shaking Jumping Mouse's
whole world.*

What is the experience of giving up an eye? What
does it mean to let go of our mouse way of perceiving?

Twenty years ago, I had a dream which indicated that 50 percent of the area in which I lived would go under water. At the time, I took the dream literally. Earth changes were quite the vogue. I was convinced the dream was an earth prophecy. The land referenced in the dream may literally one day go under water, but the more important message was the foretelling of an upcoming 50-percent change in my consciousness. I would definitely need to give up an eye. The Dream World was kind enough not to spell out the specifics of how that would unfold!

Sometimes, the "giving up of the eye" can occur only after a shock, a startling poke with the pole, which allows the space for new insight. A mother and daughter once came together for a retreat program I was conducting in England. There was a wide rift in their relationship. During the telling of their mutual stories, their psyches were poked. Disclosing previously untold parts of their individual histories allowed the possibility for a new kind of relationship to enter.

Until the program, neither the mother nor the daughter was aware of certain similarities in their childhood experiences. Ann, the mother, had been a child during World War II. Because London was so often under attack, the children of Londoners were parcelled out to relatives when possible, or to families in surrounding villages who could board children. Meanwhile, the parents stayed in the city to continue much-needed work and to maintain some sense of order and normality. The separations were painful for everyone. And visits to the country to see children were rare, since petrol was at a premium.

Ann recalled with anguish the initial, tense ride out to the countryside to her new family and the inevitable separation from her parents. What was to have been a temporary wartime situation extended into a three-year period, which was much longer than anyone had anticipated. It was an eternity for a child. The loneliness was eased, somewhat, because Ann was with her brother and they were placed with a couple who were very kind to them. Nevertheless, no matter how well-intended, her new family could never replace her real parents. She felt abandoned. An orphan child.

On one particular day, her new family announced happily, "Something wonderful is going to happen today," And, indeed it did; her mother and father came to visit! Childhood innocence returned. Ann was her real self again, happy and alive. The time with family was an enchanted interlude of warm cuddles, of walking hand-in-hand with Mom and Dad, of reading stories while sitting on comforting laps, of playing favorite games, of special talks and uproarious laughter. The magic was back!

Then, a few days later, it was over, just as suddenly as it had begun. Ann's parents announced abruptly that they had to return to London. Ann remembers being taken upstairs to her bedroom, tucked away for the night, and left alone in her room. At first, she cried silently. Then, she couldn't control the pain any longer. The sobbing became wails, deep primal moans, from a little girl with a broken heart.

Her mother rushed upstairs to her room. Ann will never forget the conversation. "I must go back to London," her mother said. "In order for me to go, you have to stop crying."

Ann's inner conflict was enormous. She wanted to please her mother she loved so dearly, and she needed to express her feelings. She made the only choice she could. She shut off her tears. Part of her died that day. She was only five.

Ironically, Katherine, Ann's daughter, had a similar trauma, also at the age of five. Katherine's father, a physician, occasionally traveled with his work. One day, when he was packing his car for a trip, something seemed different. It was unsettling and scary, an anxiety that children sense but seldom know how to articulate. Something uneasy was in the air. Something final about his departure.

No words were spoken. No explanation was given until minutes after her father had driven away. She remembers her mother sitting stoically in a rocking chair holding her baby brother, saying in a monotone voice, "Your father has left, and I don't know if he is coming back. You must be strong."

Be strong! That seemed impossible. He was the man she adored. How could she not feel? Not care? She made the only choice she could. To please her mother, she closed off her feelings. Something in her died that day, just as had happened with her mother years before.

Until that moment, neither mother nor daughter had realized that similar traumas at five caused them both to shut down emotionally. Unconscious childhood decisions had dictated their adult lives. As adults, both had issues with being able to express feelings. The mother decided that feelings are too painful. She learned to cover them up. Keep a stiff upper lip. Don't love too much. It will hurt. Katherine assumed she was responsible for her parents' separation. If she could have been nicer, if she could have been better, maybe this would not have happened. She stayed frozen in that childhood moment; part of her resisted growing up. If that is how it is to be grown up, she would simply not become an adult! Katherine became anorexic in a desperate attempt to resist maturity, to be in control in at least one area of her life.

The mother became the competent one; the daughter stayed the little girl. The mother had been irritated at her daughter for not being able to cope better; the daughter felt frustrated with the mother's demands and coldness.

Sharing the stories allowed mother and daughter to feel again. They embraced each other through heartfelt tears. A deep sisterhood began to emerge, a woman-to-woman understanding born of compassionate commonality. They both "gave up an eye." They let go of the misunderstandings about each other which had escalated through the years. The seeds of a much more genuine relationship had been firmly planted.

Then there is the story of Ellen, who had an eye of another kind to give up. During a retreat program, this time in Virginia Beach, participants were asked to spend their last afternoon in solitude. It was a time to be keenly aware of how directly the outer world reflects the inner world and to trust that what life brings to us is exactly what we need.

Ellen decided to spend her time walking barefooted on the beach and enjoying the surf of the Atlantic Ocean. She had not walked very far when she saw a multi-colored shell. Earlier in the week, it was noted in group feedback that Ellen's view of life was too polarized. She was stuck in either/or thinking. Things were either black or white, good or bad. The shell seemed to confirm her need to include more colors, more possibilities, to expand her perspective of herself and her life. She was pleased with her find.

As she continued walking, she was drawn to a lone feather lying in the sand. Not knowing why and not needing to know why, she picked up the feather and placed it in her pocket. Just as she had finished tucking away her newfound treasure, she noticed an adorable little girl, about three years old, totally absorbed in molding a figure in the sand. As she drew closer, she got a good look at the delightful fair-haired child. She had clear, sky-blue eyes, a slightly turned-up nose, and blond ringlets pulled high up on top of her head. She exuded an air of mischievousness, which made her all the more enchanting. The child, quite spontaneously, turned and smiled at the stranger. The obviously proud father sat close by, beaming, delighting in this magical child. Ellen said, "You have a beautiful little girl. Enjoy her." To which the father smiled in agreement and nodded.

Ellen flashed back to the vivid recollection of what had happened to her own little girl when she was three. Painful memories resurfaced. Like this father, Ellen had once been the adoring parent. But she had come from a severely abused childhood and was totally unprepared for parenthood. Unlike this seemingly stable father, she was an insecure, frightened mother who needed to be mothered herself.

When her daughter turned three, Ellen became afraid of her reactions to her daughter. In spite of good intentions, she found herself raging and hitting. She was repeating the same abusive behavior which she had endured. Terrified of where it might lead, she called her former husband, pleading with him to come and rescue their daughter before there was permanent damage. He took his child back. In the beginning, Ellen visited and had her daughter visit her. But circumstances changed rapidly. The father remarried and moved away and soon didn't want to share his daughter anymore with his former wife. She had, in essence, given her daughter to her husband. Legally, she had no grounds to get her daughter back. And emotionally, Ellen was too help-less to fight for visitation rights. She was too overcome with guilt and fear. Soon there was no contact at all with her daughter. The years raced. It had been fifteen years!

On her return walk on the beach, she again passed that little girl. This time the sand sculpture, which earlier had been in the beginning stages, was almost complete. With a little bit of imagination, she could clearly see the form of an angel. One of the hands was open and outstretched. Now Ellen knew what the feather was for. She gave it to the child, who smiled knowingly and promptly placed the feather in the angel's hand. It was through misty eyes that Ellen took one long last look at the little girl and waved goodbye.

As Ellen continued her walk, she saw a hotel key lodged in the sand. Intuitively, she knew exactly what the symbol was communicating. She had the key to something she had been missing for a long time!

When Ellen shared with the group that evening, she talked about the importance of the shell, the feather, the child on the beach, and the key to it all. Buffalo was asking for her eye. It was time to give up her mouse view which self-criticized and self-punished. With the new opening in her psyche, she had received new insights. She was ready, now, to do whatever it would take to be a mother and to reclaim her daughter.

By the time Ellen finished sharing her experience by the ocean, there wasn't a dry eye in the group. Some of us gave up our judgment about a mother who would abandon her child. We had eyes to give up as well.

Experiencing Synchronicity

Ellen's discoveries on the beach are examples of synchronicity, what Carl Jung calls "meaningful coincidences." It is those times when we feel a certainty that we are part of some deep oneness with the universe. At those times our outer world and our inner world unify, and the Greater Mystery lets us know when we are on track, and when we aren't! Synchronicity is a principle of the universe; thus it is always operating, even in Mouse Village. What is unique about this stage of the journey, in comparison to some earlier stage, is that by now our psyches have been "poked" somewhat. We are more able to see the Divine Play which is ever unfolding.

Sometimes the synchronistic events serve to give us confirmation that our prayers are indeed being answered. Several years ago, I suddenly developed a unexplainable longing for a rosary. Although I am not Roman Catholic, I love to pray the Rosary because of the closeness it brings to Mary. Since I was on my way to conduct a program at a Catholic convent in New York state, I decided I would purchase a rosary there. As it turned out, however, there were none for sale. When I returned home, there was a message on my answering machine from a California friend: "I have just returned from Medjugorje. The Mother told me she wants you to have a rosary. I am sending you one in the mail."

At other times, synchronistic events center around messages which Great Spirit sends in Nature. A woman on a retreat program in Hydra, Greece, had just finished processing a dream about reclaiming her feminine energy. During the break, she walked to the doorway in time to watch a giant tortoise, an ancient symbol of the feminine, cross the threshold. Nature was echoing her initiation into womanhood. What is so remarkable about the appearance of the sea turtle is that Zephra, the Retreat Center, is some 1,500 feet above sea level, and sea turtles are never seen on Hydra at that elevation!

During a retreat program in Norway, Nature brought a surprise gift to all of the participants. Originally, there was a specified limit of twelve persons for the retreat, because of the dynamics of this particular program. However, due to a mix-up in communication, thirteen persons were enrolled. Undoing the mishap would have created additional difficulties, so I agreed to include the extra person in the weekend.

The night before the retreat was to begin, I was awakened by the sounds of loud birds outside my bedroom window. I was curious as to what they were trying to communicate. The message became clear the next morning. My hostess stepped outside a moment on the balcony, which served as an extra refrigerator and which was adjacent to my bedroom. Much to her surprise, she discovered that in the early morning hours birds had broken into the cellophane package containing small loaves of bread and had meticulously taken thirteen loaves of bread, one for each participant, leaving five behind! In metaphor, birds, the messengers of Spirit, were eating bread, the beautiful light which comes from heaven. It was a clear sign that Great Spirit would be blessing each participant in a special way. Sometimes, shamans symbolically eat the shadow, or the dark negative energy, when they heal. In like manner, Great Spirit would be eating, thus transforming, each participant in the program.

The reason for thirteen participants now took on greater significance. Jesus, the thirteenth member at the Last Supper, broke bread and said, "This is my body. Eat this in remembrance of me." The number 13 also corresponds to the thirteenth path, a graduation or initiation. Once we overcome the twelve challenges, represented in the twelve houses in astrology, which are the horizontal paths in the great mandala of life, we enter the thirteenth path, the vertical path in the center of the Wheel. In Quabalistic gematria, the number 13 is the "I am" and also represents spiritual unification. It is when the Shahina is lifted, when the veil of illusion is rendered so we see God directly, face to face. The incident with the birds was Great Spirit's way of sending an affirming message to each person in the group. Each one would enter his/her sacred space, making it possible to see God more directly. That, of course, would mean coming face to face with one's own divinity.

> *Buffalo said to Jumping Mouse, "I know that you have been to the River. And I know of your quest to the Sacred Mountain. You have healed me. Because you have given so freely, I will be your brother forever. To cross the prairie, you must run under my belly. I will take you right to the foot of the Sacred Mountain. Have no fear for the spots in the sky. The eagles cannot see you while you run under me, for you will be safely hidden. All they will see is my back. I know the ways of the prairie. You are safe with me."*
>
> *Even with the confident words from Buffalo, it was frightening to be walking under a buffalo on an wide-open prairie. What about the brown spots? They were still in the sky. And the hooves were scary. What would happen if one landed on a little mouse? With only one eye, it was hard to see well enough to stay out of the way. Each time the buffalo took a step, it felt like the whole world shook. It seemed to take ever so long to walk across the prairie. But finally they stopped.*
>
> *"This is as far as I go," said Buffalo. "I am a being of the prairie. If I were to take you further, I would fall on you."*

Meetings with Buffalo

At this stage of the journey we encounter Buffalo. Buffalo are special persons who appear at auspicious moments and help take us across the prairie. They help us cross those barren places when we feel isolated and unprotected, afraid and alone.

Many years ago, when I first began my journey, I happened to quite "accidentally" come into the company of Brugh Joy, author and healer, who was in Virginia Beach for a conference. I was invited to join him in a threesome for lunch. During the course of the conversation, I had my left hand resting on the table when Brugh noticed a lapis ring I was wearing, one I had purchased in Egypt some years before. His comment about the ring triggered the spontaneous telling of a dream I had had the night before, involving the ring.

Brugh closed his eyes and went into his "Greater Brugh" self, an expanded state of awareness, which he distinguishes from his "Little Brugh," his ordinary self. From the "Greater Brugh" or Buffalo state, came some very needed insights about the dream which I had overlooked. They would help me cross my prairie. It was indeed an initiatory-level dream. How interesting that this Buffalo had appeared, just at the right moment! But then, that is the nature of Buffalo. Buffalo have impeccable timing. They know precisely how far across the prairie they should carry us and the exact place where they should stop. Though Brugh was careful to give some important clues about the dream, he was also careful not to reveal the whole symbology. The rest was for me to unravel. Unlocking the deeper levels of that dream would take several more years. But it was my task alone.

Afterwards, he said, "By the way, when you see [author and channel] David Spangler, tell him that I have been busy, so much so that I haven't been in touch, but I will write him soon."

As though there had been some mistake, I replied quickly, "Oh, I don't know David Spangler."

Nonchalantly he said, "Well, when you see him, pass this on."

It was only a week later that a friend asked me to go with him to pick up Peter Caddy, founder of Findhorn, who was speaking at a conference at the Association for Research and Enlightenment. To my astonishment, along with Peter Caddy came David Spangler, who ended up sitting next to me in the car. As Brugh requested, I passed on the message!

David smiled and said, "How like Brugh!"

We are connected in ways far beyond our knowing.

Sometimes a meeting with a Buffalo may occur without a physical meeting. We may simply hear about someone's story in a conversation and it can have impact, or we may "meet" someone in a book, or in an experience beyond this third-dimensional reality, such as in a dream or in meditation. What determines whether people are Buffalo in our lives is not whether we have seen them with our physical senses so much, but rather that they, or the energies they personify, help carry us across the prairie.

Monique had a most unusual encounter with a Buffalo. Monique is a beautiful, highly educated black woman, who lives a comfortable lifestyle. By contrast, her childhood in an inner city ghetto had been bleak. To fill the long hours when she was left alone in the apartment, Monique would sit with her face pressed against the barred window, looking out from an impoverished basement apartment, watching a strange world go by. Her mother was embarrassed by how this behavior might look to those who walked by and would scold her because she did not want her children to be seen as beggars!

Monique relished hot summer days. When the temperatures soared, the front window would stay open out of necessity, and the most aromatic smells and delectable fragrances would seep down from the apartment of a German lady two flights up. Monique would sit in the window and take deep inhalations, as though there were some unconscious, desperate hope that the smells could somehow help fill those empty places inside. The smells were goodness. It was sanity in an otherwise skewed reality. It meant somewhere there was warmth and caring and nurturing. Monique would be temporarily lifted out of her futility and the pervasive feeling of not wanting to be alive.

One imagines a blonde, stout, middle-aged *frau*, humming away, happily baking her strudel and sourdough bread in a second-floor flat. Three floors below, a dark, frail, little girl breathes as though her very life depended on it. The scintillating aroma was an umbilical cord which kept this frail child connected to life and, at the same time, lifted her spirit into another realm of possibility.

Strangely enough, Monique doesn't even remember what the German woman looked like, although she must have seen her coming in and out of the apartment. She certainly never talked to her. Nevertheless, the juncture of this nameless woman intersecting Monique's desolate existence was a foreshadowing of what would develop later as a major theme in her life. Today, as an adult, she is fascinated with food. Even the fragrances, subtleties, and delights of edible flowers have caught her fancy. It is not surprising that just as she was impacted by someone who gave her a sense of hope when there was none, Monique, now a child psychologist, offers hope to children in need. As was given to her, so she gives. Buffalo give us life that "we may have it more abundantly."

The Israeli Buffalo Woman

In my life, there have been several persons I would call Buffalo. One, whom I stumbled across on the prairie, had a major impact, even though the time spent with this person was relatively short.

Several years ago, I was in New York to give a presentation at a conference. As fate would have it, I became a last minute add-on for a dinner party in a penthouse apartment. It was a gathering where all the guests were writers or psychologists or artists, all involved, in some way, in cutting-edge thinking. The guests were expected to "sing for their supper" via meaningful conversation.

I spent the first part of the dinner talking to a psychologist who was seated on my right. Somewhere between the second and third courses, my attention turned to my left, to Dr. Jerry Epstein, author, psychiatrist, and guest of honor for the occasion. After exchanging some brief introductory remarks with Jerry, I was caught completely off guard as his tone of voice and focus of conversation completely switched. "You had a visionary experience when you were very young, didn't you?" he said, looking me right in the eye.

I almost dropped my fork. I had never met him before. He did not know me and certainly could not have had access to a very personal moment in my early life.

I was stunned. "Yes. How did you know?"

"I can read it in your face," he said. "I also had a life-changing experience, in my thirties." He referred to his teacher, a mystic, who had been extremely important in his spiritual development. When he started telling me about this eighty-year-old woman in Israel, I got a rush of energy from the top of my head to the tip of my toes. The body is the most ancient source of wisdom, one to be trusted, and that rush was a definite confirmation of a inner connection between this woman and me, one I could not ignore.

"You must go and see her," he said with authority.

I responded with an equal amount of certainty. "Yes, I will."

"January would be good."

"I can go then. I need to be in Germany the first of January. I will return home via Israel." (In retrospect, that travel route was hardly expedient, but it seemed perfectly reasonable at the time.)

"Send her your picture. Tell her I suggested you write and explain why you want to spend time with her."

I followed Jerry's suggestion and shortly thereafter received a reply from Israel and the go-ahead to continue with my plans.

Three months later, I arrived at Tel Aviv Airport. The ride from Tel Aviv to Jerusalem can be a sacred pilgrimage. As one travels the serpentine route between the two historical cities, simultaneously one winds through the delicate threads of a magnificent tapestry woven with the extraordinary colors of a rich and sacred heritage. It reflects a people with a deep faith and profound wisdom. On that particular day, however, any real appreciation of the journey was obscured by my own inner tension. Tension is a way of life in Israel. The constant threat of war keeps everyday life at a high pitch. This persuasive uneasiness, which is always in the air, as well as my travel weariness from the lengthy airplane flight culminating with the rather hostile atmosphere at the airport, combined to intensify my sudden doubts about the whole trip. There were the "could haves" to deal with. I could have stayed home and paid off my credit card. I could have researched this trip before plunging in. I could be home writing.

There were the "what ifs." What if she doesn't have much time to see me? What if my whole experience with her is a disappointment and I can't change my air ticket and leave early? What if. . .and on it went.

All concerns were born of Doubt. I was determined not to stay stuck in this state of mind. I began to dispel the doubt by going once again to the High Mountain and remembering the certainty I originally felt three months earlier in New York at the dinner party, when I first heard Collete's name. I needed to remember the universal principle that energy follows action, not the other way around. When we take a step in total trust, life responds. I reminded myself that every time I had trusted my inner feelings, life had responded. And that always, the greater the risk, the greater the benefit.

By the time the taxi arrived in Jerusalem, I was ready to enter the city and enter the experience which awaited me, whatever it might be. A quick phone call connected me with Collete. Within twenty-four hours I found myself knocking expectantly on her door and entering as the sound of a thick French Israeli accent warmly welcomed me with "Come in!"

I entered the house through an entrance hall filled with memorabilia and pictures of what appeared to be both this woman's biological family and her extended family which, no doubt, spanned the globe.

Waiting in the next room was the formidable Collete, gracefully perched on a chaise with bright Moroccan pillows plumped firmly behind her. Although she was a tiny woman, her erect posture, with her gray hair swept up high on her head and a shawl draped dramatically around her shoulders, gave her a commanding presence which defied her diminutive size. Her eyes beamed with a light that shines only in the eyes of the illumined. There sat an Israeli Buffalo woman, for sure!

"Come, sit," she said, wasting no time and pointing to a chair directly in front of her. Thus began what would be a sacred period of profound inner journeying and experiences in separate realities. Because Buffalo can dance in other realities, they are well-equipped to guide our journeys far beyond the confines of this third-dimensional world. They can dance in the fourth dimension, the psychic dimension where space as we know it does not exist and in the fifth dimension, where, mystics tell us, both space and time are transcended. And then beyond even that to the realms of archetypes and pure forms, and beyond the "beyond" to undivided wholeness. And then, in Buffalo style, they return to help us bring what comes from above so it can be planted solidly into our Earth.

It is a spiritual axiom that no one can take you deeper or higher than he has been himself. This eighty-one-year-old Jewish mystic gave unselfishly, but such is the nature of Buffalo. Country Mice, by contrast, do not have the courage to go beyond a certain point. They are restricted by their fear. But then, Collete was a Buffalo.

Despite my protests, Colette insisted there was no fee, at least on a monetary level; on the other hand, she demanded everything on a spiritual level. I am deeply grateful for her being in my life. Circumstances will perhaps preclude our meeting again. But perhaps she took me far enough.

> *"This is as far as I go, little brother," said the buffalo.*
> *"Thank you very much," said Jumping Mouse. "It was frightening crossing the prairie with only one eye. I was so afraid that one of your powerful hooves would land on me!"*
> *"You did not know, my little brother, that there was never any need for fear. For I am a Sundancer, and I*

*am always sure where my hooves land. My time with
you is over. I must go back to the prairie. You can
always find me there."*

With that, Buffalo turned and left.

Buffalo Dance Forever

When you have had a strong soul connection with
someone, the death of that person has a profound
effect. Such was my experience recently with the
passing of Paul Solomon, friend of many years, gifted
teacher, author, and channel. It was time for him to
leave and go back to the prairie. When I was informed
of Paul's death, I promptly lit a candle and kept a
flame burning for three days, as a ceremony to assist
Paul in making the transition from this life to the
next. The moment the three-day vigil was complete
and the last flickers went out from the candle, I left
Virginia Beach to present a seminar in New Orleans.
How ironic it was that this seminar was in New
Orleans, for my one visit to this magical and mysterious city had been many years before with Paul!
During that earlier trip, we were determined to experience New Orleans in grand style. There was the
late-night carriage ride through the French Quarter,
hot chocolate and beignets at the sidewalk cafe, walks
by the Mississippi River, dinner at all the best places,
jazz and more jazz, much laughter, and much joy.
We had truly celebrated life!

This trip to New Orleans was a second look at
the city, and perhaps a second look at a relationship
which had spanned some fifteen years. Just as New
Orleans is a city which contains great paradox, both
the divine and the temporal, my relationship with
Paul had included extremes, both peak experiences
and painful experiences. The relationship offered a

unique opportunity to walk through paradox and, in the end, embrace it all!

On this return visit to New Orleans I was sitting at the very sidewalk cafe where I had once been with Paul, once again enjoying hot chocolate and beignets, this time with my good friend Lynne. On this visit, rather than talking to Paul I was talking about him. Lynne had never known Paul, but as we sat and talked, it seemed appropriate that we would share in a final ceremony to honor this remarkable man. We agreed we would go together to St. Louis King of France Cathedral, which was nearby, and offer our prayers. What I wanted most was to ask the Mother to heal Paul's wounded child and to take away the pain of this man who had been the Good Shepherd to so many souls. No sooner had we agreed on the ceremony than an elementary school teacher, with students by her side, made her way to our table. There were no free tables and she wondered if we might share the extra chairs placed at our table with some of her children. Three little boys promptly took their seats with us. How appropriate that it be young boys in light of our conversation about Paul's inner child. One little boy rather dramatically propped his elbow on the table, positioned his head on his fist, and looked directly at me, as though to convey a message beyond words. "Do I know you?" he asked quizzically.

"Well," I said, smiling, "you do now!"

Hot chocolate and beignets consumed, Lynne and I crossed over to St. Louis' and entered the cathedral door. It was late afternoon, that numinous period when light gives way gently to the approaching mystery of the night, when what is known surrenders to what is unknown. We happened upon a quiet time in the church. A lone person, a man, sat by himself in a pew. I gave him only a momentary glance, noticing only the back of his head, for our attention was focused on the statue of Mary directly ahead. Once we made our way to the front of the church, we each lit a candle and knelt in prayer before the peaceful, welcoming arms of the Mother. After spending some time in a meditative mode, we walked back down the aisle and found the man still sitting in prayer. Only this time I managed to get a closer look at him. He was dressed in a red clerical collar with a large gold cross hung around his neck. What startled me was that he looked exactly as Paul did some fifteen years ago when we first met. I was stunned. It may have been an apparition. Or it may have been an amazing synchronistic event, that the one person sitting in the church when we were praying for Paul would resemble him so perfectly. Either way, the point was made. I knew that Paul, who had given me and others so much in life, was still giving, and would continue to give, this time from the higher realms.

Immediately after we stepped outside the church, a group of school boys ran up to us. They were happy children, laughing, playing, spontaneous, alive, vulnerable, trusting. I knew with certainty now that Paul was a happy child again, just as he had once been in New Orleans. No doubt, he was still celebrating life!

Buffalo continue to help others cross the prairie, even when they are in another dimension. This mighty Buffalo was still dancing. For Buffalo dance forever!

CHAPTER SIX

Inner Knowing

*J*umping Mouse was happy in his new surroundings. There were new things to investigate. There were plants in abundance and new seeds to enjoy. As he was busy exploring this new place, suddenly before him was a gray wolf. The wolf didn't seem to see the little mouse. In fact, he didn't seem to be seeing much of anything. He was just sitting there, doing nothing.

Jumping Mouse was pleased to find a new friend in the woods and spoke to him right away. "Hello, Brother Wolf."

Immediately, the wolf's ears sat up and he became alert. He looked directly at Jumping Mouse. "Am I a wolf? Yes, that is what I am. Wolf! Wolf! I am a wolf!" He seemed quite pleased with his new discovery. But then his mind dimmed again, and in a matter of minutes he had forgotten completely who he was!

Several times the same sequence occurred. The wolf would just sit, quietly staring out into nothingness, completely without memory as to who he was. Jumping Mouse would say, "But you are a mighty being. You are a wolf."

"Yes," would come the answer from the gray wolf. "I am a wolf! Yes, now I remember. That is what I am!" He would become excited once again, but soon would forget again.

"Such a great being," thought Jumping Mouse, "but he has no memory. He has forgotten who he is."

Meeting the Wise Innocent

The Wolf is the guardian of the threshold to the Sacred Mountain. He presents a paradox, for he is both an obstacle and the entry way to the mountain. The Wolf is akin to the Fool in the tarot. Within the tarot deck of cards is an ageless and ubiquitous representation of the archetypal journey. There are seventy-eight cards in all, with twenty-two major arcana cards, each with pictures which symbolically depict man's spiritual journey. The first card in the deck, and one of the major arcana, is one called the Fool, the Wise Innocent, who illustrates a reality beyond appearance.

In the tarot, the Fool is the most powerful of all the tarot trumps. He appears at the beginning of the journey and again at the end of the journey. He is both the Alpha and the Omega, the beginning and ending of manifestation. Unlike the other tarot cards, the Fool has no fixed number. Sallie Nichols explains, "The zero or 'nothing' is really something, and this 'nothing' occupies space and contains power." Because the Fool is the zero in the deck, he is free to travel at will, often in a way which creates havoc in the established order.

The Fool is most definitely an archetype to be reckoned with, one we meet in many guises. We must deal with him when he reveals himself in our inner world, and we must confront him when he appears in our outer world. In history and in literature, we learn of him in numerous portrayals. He is the Clown, the Court Jester, the Joker, the Kashari, the Trickster, and the Unexpected Messenger. He is Mishkin in Dostoevski's *The Idiot,* Parsifal in *The Holy Grail*, and Edgar, the alter ego, in Shakespeare's *King Lear.*

In *King Lear,* the central figure, rendered blind and helpless, must wander, aimlessly exposed to the wild rages of an untamed tempest from within and without. It takes Edgar, disguised as a fool, to guide Lear through a reconciliation of the extremes which in turn enables him to eventually assume a kingly clarity. Paradoxically, the way to true sanity is often through the safe passage between childishness and madness. The Fool can masterfully play the seductive devil, luring us to madness; at the same time, he is the potential Savior who helps us find our way to salvation. In the A.E. Waite tarot deck, the symbolical representation of the Fool reflects the opposites he embraces. On the one hand is the Innocent. His garments are flowered. There is a knapsack slung over his shoulder, and he carries a rose in his left hand. He is an androgenous being, a happy blend of both masculine and feminine qualities. Looming in front of him is a dangerous precipice, but in spite of the impending danger (the madness that he is one step away from) the young Fool prances along without a care. His head is tilted upwards, sheathed in cloudy dreams, oblivious to harm, with a heart which longs for romance and adventure. Like Parsifal in *The Holy Grail*, he is naive. He has no notion of what question to ask of life or even if one is required. By his side is a little dog, his instinctual self, the primal power of the Creator, who can both sense danger and help him avoid it. The Fool's redemption lies in his innate simplicity and trust. He fears nothing, for he knows that he is always guided and protected. He trusts God implicitly. And like all fools, he somehow survives, in spite of himself, for he has been touched by the Hand of God.

It is that very simplicity and trust which is required for one to be allowed entrance into the Sacred Mountain, the Heart of God within ourselves. When we meet the Wolf, our tendency might be to dismiss, negate, or avoid him altogether. After all, the Wolf has no memory. He is just a fool! But to dismiss the Wolf would mean that we would not find the Mountain and never fully discover our intuitive and compassionate selves.

The Magus of Strovolos, otherwise known as Daskalos, the amazing Cyprian healer, speaks of the three attributes of the Absolute: total wisdom, total power, and total goodness (what he also calls love). They are likewise the attributes within ourselves that must come into balance. In Nature, which is the macrocosm, the triangle is always balanced. In the microcosm within ourselves, however, the inner triangle is often an isosceles triangle, a triangle in the process of becoming isometric and balanced. At this stage of one's journey, it is quite possible that a person may have acquired both knowledge and power. But Daskalos warns about the necessity of acquiring the third quality, goodness (or love). He says that when an individual has only knowledge and power and lacks goodness (or love), a Satanic condition prevails. A demon is, after all, an "incomplete god." The closer one is to balancing his triangle, the closer one is to self-realization.

"Except Ye Become as a Little Child"

Jumping Mouse looked at the wolf and saw that he had no memory. But he also knew the wolf to be "a great being." Jumping Mouse looked at the wolf the way a child sees, with goodness, with pure innocence and an open heart. Jesus said, "Except ye become as a little child, ye shall not enter the kingdom of heaven."

I am reminded of Annie, a little girl who lives in Atlanta, Georgia, who, like Jumping Mouse, was able to see the Wolf when it crossed her path. Annie had that extraordinary quality of goodness which enabled her to see into the hearts of people and help them remember who they are. Why, Annie could even see inside stuffed animals! A conversation once overheard between Annie and her Mother went something like this:

"Oh, Annie, you have so many stuffed animals. Why, I can hardly find you in bed at night because of all your animals."

"Mom, to you they may just be stuffed animals. But to me, they have heart and soul."

With such a compassionate heart, it is not surprising that all of Annie's friends, including those stuffed with cotton, held important places in her life. But of her many friends, it was Jason to whom she was most loyal. For Jason was, according to Annie, her best friend and the "kindest person I know."

Seeing the two of them together was sheer delight. It was a magical blend, indeed! There would be Jason, smiling broadly, towering at least six inches over the head of his little Annie, who, in turn, would be looking up adoringly at her trusted friend. At times, you could catch glimpses of them playing their favorite game, He-Rah and She-Rah. They would spend endless hours chasing happily about, exuding joy and laughter, arrayed in homemade costumes, complete with flowing capes, wands, and sparkling headgear.

Jason and Annie attended the same school. There, however, the inseparable twosome were apart. In fact, they seldom saw one another, for Annie was placed in the gifted program for high-achievers while Jason was placed in a special education class for the mentally impaired.

In their neighborhood, there was predictable chatter about Jason. Parents were concerned about the effect

Jason might have on their "normal" children. Annie, however, like Parsifal, was not concerned about conventional good manners and the advice of elders. She was guided more by feelings, the "language of God to the soul." Annie could see inside Jason in a way that others could not. Just being around Annie somehow made it easier for others to see as well. When parents saw how much Annie cared for Jason and that being with him had not slowed her down, even one bit, they began to change their views. In time, Annie gave many people an appreciation of Jason.

And it was Annie who could help Jason "remember" who he was, especially during those times when he would get discouraged. "Come on, Jason, you can do it! I know you can." And somehow, assured by Annie's words, he would manage what, for him, had seemed the impossible.

When Annie was nine, Jason and his family moved away from the neighborhood. It was a sad farewell for two devoted friends. As a going-away gift, Jason gave Annie a "gold" ring. Of course, she would sometimes need to wash off the band of black which would appear on her finger underneath the ring. Nevertheless, for several years, that ring remained her most precious possession.

Mother Teresa was once asked, "There are so many people in India who are in need. What is it that one can give to them?"

Her response was, "Give them their dignity." I think Annie would understand.

Jumping Mouse would help the wolf remember who he was for a moment, but then he would forget again. Jumping mouse wanted to help his new friend. "If giving up an eye could help the buffalo, then maybe I could give up my eye to the wolf and he would be well, too." This time there was no hurrying and scur-rying around. And there was no need to ask anyone else for advice. He knew how to find his own answer. This time, he went to a peaceful spot and sat quietly. In the silence, he listened to his heart. It told him exactly what he must do.

To enter the Sacred Mountain, we first must see, or recognize, the Wolf, as did Annie, and then we must heal the Wolf. The Wolf is that aspect of ourselves who forgets who we are. We are gods and goddesses with amnesia. We momentarily forget our true nature. . .our divinity. As we see and heal our Wolf selves, we unleash our own instinctual selves. As with Parsifal, the Fool's connection with his instinctual side has the potential to save not only himself but all humankind.

I remember a story Elizabeth Kubler Ross shared. The story went something like this. . .She was travel-ing by herself somewhere in Europe, not as Elizabeth Kubler Ross, noted psychiatrist and authority on death and dying, but simply as a woman, traveling alone, like many others, with no special identity.

She arrived at the train station in plenty of time before departure and looked for a place to sit. Her attention was immediately drawn to a forlorn-looking boy, about thirteen years old, sitting slumped over on one end of a bench. He was overwhelmed with sadness. . .He had forgotten who he was.

So as not to disturb him, she sat down on the far end of the same bench. Her heart reached out to the young boy. Nothing was said; nothing needed to be said.

She sat for a long time in the silence, listening within. After a long, pregnant pause, she said simply, "Rough, huh?"

The youth nodded, mumbling a weak, "Yup."

They sat for some fifteen or more minutes, communicating nonverbally. She sat, as did Jumping Mouse, listening to her heart. It told her exactly what to do.

"That rough, huh?" she said.

"Yup."

With that, he slowly lifted his shirt up to expose a back with raised welts, still raw and red, evidence of a brutal beating from his father.

She sensed the moment and slid over on the bench, to sit closer to the boy. At least an hour remained before the train would come. She would know what to share. It would probably be the most important hour in this young boy's life. And perhaps it was a special hour for Elizabeth Kubler Ross, for all healing is self-healing.

Giving Up Another Eye

Wasting no time, Jumping Mouse hurried back to where the wolf was.

"Brother Wolf," he called out.

"Wolf? Wolf?" came the still-confused response.

"Brother Wolf, listen to me. I know now what will heal you. If I could give an eye to a buffalo and it would heal him, then I will gladly give you my eye."

No sooner had he said the words than the last eye of the little mouse flew out of his head. Now Jumping Mouse had no eyes. But that didn't seem to matter so much. What mattered was that the wolf was whole again. He could remember who he was.

Giving up the last eye requires us to surrender those remaining limited parts of self which prevent us from being able to totally trust within. Once we begin to listen with our hearts as did Jumping Mouse with the wolf, we must expect inner changes and, in all probability, outer changes as well. Most likely, the world we consider safe, familiar, and reliable may suddenly be shattered or be turned upside-down. And this shift can occur in the twinkling of an eye. The dramatic changes, the flip-flops, the sudden turn-arounds, the wrenching away from what we have thought was our security, all serve the greater purpose: to shift our focus from reliance on the outer to trust in the inner.

The story of the initiation of one man, Frederic Lionel, is told through a tale of espionage and true adventure in *Challenge: On Special Mission*. Frederic was living in France at the beginning of World War II when Germany suddenly invaded France. The world he relied on ceased to be. Frederic, a Frenchman who was fluent in German, offered his services to the British Government to initiate a rescue service for those wanting to escape from France to England. He was one of the first to develop a link between the Fifth Column and the Underground Movement in France. Thus began four years of high-level espionage work with the Underground Movement in France.

His book, at one level, is a gripping tale of adventure and intrigue. But at its most profound level, it is an account of the demanding training of an initiate. Frederic went through hair-raising adventures in order to make a breakthrough in consciousness. Through his experiences, he developed a highly sensitized intuition which eventually would enable him to instantly respond with total obedience to the promptings of the still, small voice within his own mind and heart. Not only his life, but the lives of many came to depend on his ability to trust solely in an invisible guidance which worked through the very center of his consciousness.

Seeing With No Eyes

Not everyone is required to experience war settings to learn total trust in the Higher Self. Experiences vary from person to person and seemingly are tailor-made to the precise needs of each individual. The circumstance in which one finds oneself are not what matters so much. What does matter is that one makes the shift from dependence on the limited sensory world of this third-dimensional reality to trust instead in the world of Spirit and the higher dimensions where we see with no eyes. It is here that we see with inner sight, a knowing born of compassion, intuition, and discernment. Like Jumping Mouse, we listen with our heart and know exactly what to do.

One who "sees with no eyes" is my dear friend, Ann Maria. When I worked as a cancer therapist many years ago, there were times when I felt that I needed more insight about certain patients in order to be of greater value. When I needed confirmation in pinpointing a deeply veiled core issue, or simply when I needed extra help with a patient, I would call on Ann Maria, who at that time lived in New York. I would set up a three-way phone conversation: Ann Maria, me, and an exceptional nine-year-old boy who also "sees with no eyes." When I gave them the name of a particular patient, they would then proceed to see that person, not with physical sight but with spiritual sight. They would describe the patient and illness, as well as the underlying cause of the illness, and suggest possible methods of helping the patient. In addition, they always offered prayers for the patient and his family. Ann Maria preferred being anonymous. The patients were never told about the unseen help they were receiving. But they were frequently puzzled by the sudden and often dramatic changes in their conditions.

Even as a child, Ann Maria could see in ways that others could not. One day, when Ann Maria was seven, she was spending time alone in the flower garden behind her house. A large white rose caught her attention. She picked the rose, being careful not to disturb its beauty, and then proceeded to sit on the grass and enjoy its exquisite form. She became aware of a soft, warm light from above which began to shine directly on the roses's fragile petals. The rose began to glow with an effervescent light. And the air was filled with the special ambiance of a pungent yet delicate scent.

Suddenly, in her peripheral vision,, she saw the sandaled feet of someone standing nearby. Although this stranger appeared unexpectedly, she was not frightened. He brought only peace. Her eyes moved from his sandals to the hem of his robe and then upwards. He was dressed as a Franciscan monk, in a long, dark-brown cloak, loosely belted at the waist with a knotted cord. A shawl collar framed a young man's face with eyes so compassionate that they could look deep inside, all the way to the soul. It was a look which never invaded, only loved.

She asked the stranger, in her childlike innocence, how he was able to be there. He just smiled. He took a step forward, took his hands out of his robe, pushed his right sleeve up slightly, and then placed his hand on the top of her head and blessed her. Her first communion would be in a few days. She wondered if he had come to celebrate this special event. When he was through blessing her, she offered him her rose. He smiled and graciously received her gift. With rose in hand, he disappeared, just as suddenly as he had first appeared.

Somehow she knew to "hide these things in her heart," in the Biblical sense. Only her father was privy to what had happened. He confirmed what she already knew: "Keep it to yourself!" As a young Catholic, Ann Maria knew the names and stories of many saints. She assumed the familiar stranger was St. Francis, even though the face of the man in the garden was not quite how she had pictured St. Francis. It was not until years later, when she took a pilgrimage to Capuchin Monastery in San Giovanni Rotondo at Foggia, Italy, that she knew the true identity of the person who had appeared years earlier in the garden. When she walked into the Rotondo of the monastery, there stood the same monk who had blessed her as a child. He was with the other monks, greeting the fifty or so persons who were gathered for Mass. His face was older, and he had grown a beard, but his eyes were unmistakably the same eyes she had seen as a child—kind, compassionate, and infinitely loving. She knew him, now, to be Padre Pia, a remarkable Italian monk. His words to her were, "I have been expecting you."

Ann Maria eventually learned that Padre Pia had accepted her and two other motherless children to be his Spiritual Children in 1918, the year Ann Maria's mother died. Unknown to Ann Maria, she had lost her mother and had been adopted at the same moment. Padre Pia recorded Ann Maria's name, her date of birth, and the name of her mother in a diary, which was a record of his revelations. (This information was documented and later sent to Ann Maria following Padre Pia's death.) Padre Pia had never been told anything about a little girl born in Brooklyn, New York. How could he possibly have known the needs of a child who lived all the way across a vast ocean? How little we know of the mysteries!

Padre Pia was said to have had many gifts, including bi-location, the ability to be in two locations simultaneously, which Ann Maria witnessed as a child, as well as the gifts of healing, prophecy, levitation, discernment, perfumes, and stigmata. Perhaps it is because of the blessing from Padre Pia, or perhaps for reasons quite unrelated to him, Ann Maria has many of these same gifts herself.

The term *hypertext* has been used to explain the process whereby you push one button and the entire range of information about a subject becomes available, as if it were a computer data base. Ann Maria describes her process of knowing in slightly different terms; she speaks of going "behind the veil" or going "into the silence." From that deep, still place of total trust within come the revelations, the positive knowings.

Not all of those who see with no eyes are mystics as are Padre Pia and Ann Maria. But there is a distinctive quality about people who are at this stage of the journey. They have a rare combination of both a highly developed intuitive sense and an enormous capacity for love.

Some years ago, when I was at a critical juncture in my life, my Aunt Nita, my father's sister, unexpectedly called from Washington, D.C. I hadn't heard from her in two years, so it was most auspicious that she would pick that particular night to call!

"Betty, I just had to call you tonight. Something told me to do so. I just want you to know how much you are loved. You are a part of our family and you always have a place in my home and in my heart." Tears ran down my face. Like the Wolf, I had been forgetting who I was. I needed a reminder. I could hear both my earthly father, deceased now for some years, and my Heavenly Father speaking through her. The timing was perfect. How like Aunt Nita to call at this moment. Even as a child, I was aware of her ability to know things others were not aware of.

As it turned out, I had an upcoming conference in Washington, and, even though I had already made reservations at a hotel, the synchronistic call signaled the need for an abrupt change of plans. I looked forward to this opportunity to stay with my aunt, for, as a child, staying with my aunts in the big city was a highlight of the summer. There was Chinatown, movies, restaurants, shopping, and amusement parks. It didn't seem to matter what we did; it was always fun! Aunt Nita was ninety-four now, and blind. She shared her home with her half-sister, my Aunt Alice Mae, who was now in her seventies. And I would be with them again, after all these years.

When I pulled in front of their house on Shepherd Street, I was stunned. Had it shrunk? Surely, the house was bigger than this. As a child I had thought this two-story, four-bedroom structure enormous. The yard had been a child's wonderland, with nooks and crannies that lent themselves as secret hiding places where one could go undetected during Hide and Seek. By contrast, now the yard looked quite manicured and the house certainly ample, but no way near the proportions I remembered.

Inside, very little had changed. Just as I had remembered, there was the rose-colored carpet, the marble fireplace, the same draperies, now slightly faded, and the carefully positioned furniture. In the bedroom where I used to sleep was the same rose-pink, floral wall paper and the tiny ballerina on the porcelain bed-side lamp, which when I was a child would dance me to sleep each night.

And Aunt Nita, a widow for some years now, was still as warm-hearted, outrageous, and funny as ever! Alice Mae, with incredible patience and dedication, tried to keep Aunt Nita in tow. They were a delightful "odd couple" indeed!

"How are you doing, Betty?" came the warm welcome from Aunt Nita. "It is so good to see you.

You are looking wonderful. Of course, I can't see a thing, but I know you are doing fine!" And out came one of her contagious belly laughs.

Although her spirit was intact, age had taken its toll. Aunt Nita's body was stooped, and she walked with the aid of a walker. What little hair she had left was concealed under a turban which she insisted Alice Mae place on her head. "Now, how do you like my hat? Isn't that something? I just wanted to dress up when I knew you were coming." Again, more warm-hearted laughter.

As we sat down in the living room to catch up on talk about her children, grandchildren, great-grandchildren and her church, as well as what was what was wrong in the White House (all her favorite subjects), the conversation was interrupted by a phone ringing.

"Alice Mae, get the phone!" came the direct orders of Aunt Nita.

Alice Mae responded in her gentle way, "Did the phone ring? I didn't hear it!"

To which Aunt Nita said, "Honestly, they think I am deaf and they think I am blind, but I have to tell them when the phone rings and what is going on!" And there would be more light-hearted laughter.

In the morning I said a hurried goodbye and rushed off to a full day of conference activities. When I returned that evening, I made a point to be early. Trying to be considerate of their advanced age, I turned the key at shortly after 10:00 PM, expecting to find the house quiet and everyone sound asleep. Instead, things were buzzing! Lights were on, Aunt Nita was on the phone, laughing and talking, and Alice Mae was busily engaged in some project of her own. "What are you doing home so early?" they asked.

"I thought you might be asleep. I didn't want to disturb you."

"Oh, for heaven's sake, no! We are just a bunch of gypsies around here. We are liable to go to bed almost anytime. We do what we want to do!" And reels of more laughter.

Aunt Nita and I had one last talk before I left Washington. "Now, Betty, your father told me many years ago that I would live to be ninety-five," she said. "Your father was right about most things, and I have known for some time he is right about this too. So, in case I don't see you again, on this side, I will see you on the other."

With that, I went up to Aunt Nita so I could pour my love into her with one last hug. I wanted to etch her clearly in my memory, the way one might do who has no physical eyes. I placed my fingers gently on her face and began to trace her high check bones, her marvelously smooth brow, the slight indentation in the center of the forehead, the noble, straight nose, and the firm jawline. So many feelings surfaced. Her head was almost identical to that of my father. And I had touched his head in similar fashion just before he died.

Aunt Nita's last words to me were, "It was wonderful seeing you again." Of course, she hadn't seen me with physical eyes, but then she had seen me. And she had given me an "eye." It was her love that helped me remember who I was.

As soon as the eye of the mouse went into the wolf, he was healed.

Tears started to flow down the wolf's face. Of course, Jumping Mouse could not see him because he had no eyes. He was blind. But even without eyes, he could see that the wolf was whole again. Now, the wolf could remember who he was.

"Thank you, Jumping Mouse, for healing me."

CHAPTER SEVEN

With the Eyes of an Eagle

"*You* have healed me," said the wolf, as tears ran down his cheeks. "Thank you, my little friend. Now I can remember many things. I am the guide to the Sacred Mountain and to the Great Medicine Lake. And it is your time to go there. You are blind, so you must follow close beside me. But I know the way, and I will take you there."

The wolf, with his little friend close beside, slowly made his way through the tall pine trees to the edge of the Sacred Lake. Unlike the river which roared as it rushed over rocks, the lake sat in perfect stillness. "This lake," said the wolf, "is more powerful even than the mighty river. For this is a Medicine Lake. It reflects all the world, all the people of the world, the lodges of the people, and all the beings of the prairies and the skies. It is said that he who drinks of this Sacredness is given the wisdom to understand the mysteries of life."

Jumping Mouse leaned down and drank the cool, refreshing water from the Sacred Lake.

The wolf said, "This is where I must leave you, little friend, for I must return. There are others I must guide. But if you want, I will stay with you for a while."

"Thank you, my brother, but you must go, and it is my time to be alone." Even though Jumping Mouse was trembling with fear, he said goodbye to his friend.

*Jumping Mouse stood alone and trembling, sens-
ing what was to come. He knew, somehow, that an
eagle would find him. All of a sudden he could feel a
shadow on his back. Then he heard the noise of a giant
eagle swooping down, coming closer. He braced himself for what was to come. . .the noise grew louder, an
enormous swoosh. . .then, a thump on his back. Jumping Mouse fell into a deathlike sleep.*

The Final Surrender

In many of the ancient traditions, in the myths
and in the legends, the hero/heroine falls into an
deathlike sleep just prior to the final initiation. In
the myth *Eros and Psyche,* Psyche must descend into
the underworld to complete her final challenges as
a mortal. Her last task is to bring back an unopened
vial of beauty ointment to Aphrodite, with a strict
admonition not to open the vial. Psyche encounters
the paradox: does she listen within or do as she is
told? She follows her own promptings and opens the
flask. Immediately she falls into a deathlike sleep.
Alas, it appears that all is lost. Paradoxically, just
the opposite is true. She passes her final initiation
because she both demonstrated trust in her own inner
authority above all other authority and demonstrated
the discernment to know the right timing and the
right action. If either action or timing were amiss,
she would have failed the initiation. Psyche is sub-
sequently lifted out of her deathlike sleep and taken
to Mt. Olympus, where she, no longer a mortal, is
transformed into a goddess.

In the Christian Mysteries, Jesus was placed in a
tomb for three days, after which he overcame death
and was resurrected into a new life. Likewise, in the
Egyptian mysteries, the initiates lay in state, again

for a three-day period, and demonstrated mastery over death and this third-dimensional reality by leaving their physical bodies and traveling into other dimensions. And mystics in many traditions describe a "dark night of the soul," a deathlike period of total isolation and desperation before their final illumination.

When don Juan pushes Carlos Castenada into another state of being, he hits him in the back between the shoulder blades with the palm of his hand. In a sense it is a death, death to the limited Carlos and the resurrection of the awakened Carlos. Likewise, when the eagle swooshes down and hits Jumping Mouse, the touch of the eagle induces him to fall asleep into the nether world.

"We make vessels of clay," observed Lao-tzu, "but their true nature is in the emptiness within." To contact this natural emptiness is the object of the spiritual practices in many traditions. We return to the place of the inexhaustible well of silence. It is from that still, primal silence that existed before the first word of creation that we replenish our spirit. To find a new creative word, we must plumb the primal silence and return to that point of light before thought.

T.S. Eliot, in *Four Quartets*, so poignantly expresses this state of total emptiness:

> I said to my soul, be still, and wait without hope
> For hope would be hope for the wrong thing; wait without love
> For love would be love of the wrong thing; there is yet faith
> But the faith and the love and the hope are all in the waiting;
> Wait without thought, for you are not ready for thought;
> So the darkness shall be the light, and the stillness the dancing.

Joseph Rael describes darkness as the "blowing breath that has eyes to see." Darkness is a profound teacher. One can learn something of her mysteries in the countries of the Far North. Norway, land of the midnight sun, has a compelling beauty, especially in the dead of winter when there are precious few hours of daylight. When we are unaccustomed to this more somber side of nature, the preponderance of darkness feels unfamiliar and hauntingly strange. It can be threatening, for we are conditioned with negative images about nighttime and darkness. Once we become accustomed to a world where nature is black and gray and diffuse, unformed and unknown, we gradually embrace the darkness. Within it we discover great peace. Black is the Deeper Self, the Breath, the Great Mystery, the Divine Feminine, the Infinite Void from which all comes. It teaches us to let go, to surrender, and to "give up our last eye." No need to know. No concern about past, no worry about the future. Only trust. Only the moment. The exquisite state of no thought. Silence. Being.

Entering the Stillness

"The Journey Into Silence" is a short story to tell but it can be a very long story to live. Like Jumping Mouse, one begins the journey in a rather bewildered state. It takes some time before one can trust the innermost stirrings of the heart and move through expectations, words, thoughts, and emotions to the silence which is at the center of the self. A favorite Zen story says it well.

A young man once approached a Master. "Master," he said, "I want to learn about wisdom. Would you teach me the way?"

"You may accompany me on my way, if you so choose," the Master replied.

"Oh, thank you, Master!" said the pleased disciple.

The two set out, walking together in silence. It wasn't very long before they entered a very dense forest. They continued walking. Again, no words were spoken.

The disciple began to lose his patience and become quite irritated. "The old man is walking so slowly," he thought to himself. "We will never get anywhere! Besides, he promised to teach me the way to wisdom. How can I learn anything like this? Days have gone by, and he has not said one word to me! What kind of a teacher is he?"

At that moment, the Master stopped abruptly and turned to the disciple. "What do you hear?" he asked.

"Hear?" replied a disgusted disciple. "I do not hear anything in this miserable forest!"

To that, the old man simply nodded. And continued on his way.

They walked on and on, without saying another word. Again, the Master stopped. "What do you hear now?" he asked.

"I hear something very beautiful! I hear the songs of a thousand birds and the wind making music in the trees!" the disciple exclaimed. "Why, this forest is full of life! Master, thank you for bringing me to this wonderful place. Let us stay here."

The old man simply nodded. And continued on his way.

They walked together, in silence. This time they walked for a very long time. At length, the Master stopped. "Now, what do you hear?" he asked.

"I hear the babbling of the brook. The sound comforts me," the disciple replied.

The old man nodded. And continued on his way.

They continued to walk together in silence, on and on, deeper and deeper into the forest. Then the Master paused again. "What do you hear now?" he asked.

This time the disciple whispered, "I hear the silence at the center of the forest. All is peace."

The old man said nothing, only nodded. And continued on his way.

They walked on in the silence together for what may have been many years. Then, one day, the Master stopped. He turned to the disciple and asked, "What do you hear now?"

The disciple turned toward the Master and smiled gently. This time he said nothing. Instead, he bowed to his Master.

And the Master then bowed to his disciple. "I will no longer have to accompany you on your way," he said.

The disciple nodded. And continued his way. Alone.

Becoming an Eagle

The metaphor of total surrender and the full awakening to the transcendent reality is beautifully enacted during the Picuris Pueblo Pole-Climbing Ceremony, in Northern New Mexico. This ceremony takes place annually on Feast Day, August 10. In the center of the pueblo stands an enormous wooden pole, towering at around fifty feet, which has been made from a fallen tree stripped of bark and limbs. Tied to the top of the pole is the carcass of a dead sheep (foundation of life), a watermelon (embracing betrayal), and loaves of bread (beautiful light). Every year, a *kashari* (*pa-wai-eh na* in Tiwa), also known as a clown, climbs the pole. In metaphor, the one who climbs the pole keeps the channels open to the Higher Realms. He is also the one who brings down abundance for the community and for the people.

As a preliminary to the pole-climbing ceremony, the *kashari,* with bodies and faces covered in black and white, entertain with their antics. The clown is the ubiquitous joker, the fool who is a combination of wisdom, madness, and folly. At every possible opportunity, the clowns embarrass and shock people. They make others both laugh at themselves and laugh at others. When the pole-climbing begins, everyone laughs at the clowns as they make their purposely foolish attempts to climb the pole and then fall down, over and over again. On one level, we can dismiss the clowns. They are just being silly. Maybe they have lost their memory, as did the wolf. They don't seem to know who they are.

But the clown teaches us that appearance and reality are not synonymous. See through the illusion. The world that we see is not what we perceive it to be! Just when we are convinced that what the clowns are doing is just buffoonery, one of the clowns begins to seriously climb the mammoth pole. He pulls with both arms, using his legs to brace himself and in that manner shimmies rhythmically up the pole. It is a breathtaking sight to see—ancient, primal, alive! As the clown ascends the pole, metaphorically he is going up the various levels of consciousness.

Each year it is the same ceremony and each year it is a different ceremony. During a recent Feast Day, one of the clowns made it halfway up the pole and then suddenly stopped climbing. It would seem that he had the physical prowess to go the rest of the way, yet he simply stopped. He placed his head against the pole, and his mouth was moving, as though he were speaking with Spirit for permission to continue the climb. He had reached an impasse. Like Jumping Mouse, he had entered a void, a darkness, an abyss which he could not cross. He came down and attempted the climb again. The same thing occurred. Again, he was blocked from going any higher. The portal of the gates of the higher dimensions was closed. It was not his time; he was not the one to complete the climb. He came down the pole and another *kashari* took his place. This time when the same spot in the pole was reached, the portals opened and he climbed effortlessly all the way through the impasse to the top, to the higher realms of consciousness, beyond form, to the state of emptiness. The *kashari,* the clown, the fool, both the alpha and the omega, takes us to Nothing, to zero, the perfect symbol of the state of undivided wholeness before the creation of things. This nothing is outside time and space. It is pure nature, pure being, the essence behind the veil.

When a *kashari* reaches the top, all eyes are fixed on the pole. Perched high on top, the *kashari* confidently unties the ropes (being watchful of thoughts) and lets down the sheep, the bread, and the watermelon to the people below. His majestic form is dramatically silhouetted against an open blue sky. He is fluid yet solid, graceful yet powerful. At this point in the ceremony, he no longer seems the clown; he has been transformed into another form. From that high place, he looks more like an eagle, a Great Being who is at home in the clouds, at home in the Mind of God!

Much to Jumping Mouse's surprise, he began to awaken. The surprise of being alive was great. And he could see! Even though everything was blurry, he could see colors and they were beautiful.

"I can see! I can see!" said Jumping Mouse over again and again.

A blurry shape started to move near Jumping Mouse. Jumping Mouse squinted hard, trying to see, but the shape remained a blur.

"Hello, brother," a familiar voice said. "Do you want some medicine?"

"Some medicine? Me? Yes! Yes!"

"Then," said the voice, "what you must do is crouch down as low as you can, and jump as high as you can."

Jumping Mouse did exactly what he was told. He crouched as low as he could and jumped as high as he could! Suddenly, a wind caught him and began to lift him higher and higher.

"Do not be afraid," the assuring voice called out. "Ride the wind. Hang on to it. It will carry you. . .TRUST!"

Jumping Mouse did as he was told. He closed his eyes and let go. The wind began to carry him. The wind, the breath of Great Spirit, lifted him higher and higher. This time, when Jumping Mouse opened his eyes, they were clear. The higher he went, the clearer they became. He could see with the eyes of an eagle. He could see through things and into things. He could see miles away. He could see in the Spirit Way.

As Jumping Mouse looked down, way below was his old familiar friend. There was the frog, sitting on a lily pad on the beautiful medicine lake.

"You have a new name," called the frog. "You are no longer Jumping Mouse. You are Eagle!"

So ends the story of Jumping Mouse. May you find yourself somewhere in this journey. May you see with new eyes.

May Your Heart be Opened and May your Spirit Soar like the Eagle!

The Story of Jumping Mouse

Once there was a mouse named Jeremy who, like all the other mice, lived in a little village hidden away in the woods. He was always busy, doing the things that mice do, running and jumping, looking and searching, hurrying and scurrying, to and fro. It seemed he was always in motion. In fact, he hardly ever stood still. And, like the other mice, he couldn't see very far. Nor was he able to see very clearly. For mice, as you may have noticed, usually have their whiskers in the ground.

One day Jeremy began to hear a new strange sound, one he had not heard before. It was a roar coming from somewhere out in the distance. Now Jeremy was used to the sounds of the forest. He knew the different sounds of the two-legged and the four-legged and the winged and the hoofed. But this was unlike anything he had known.

Sometimes, he would stop everything and lift his head to the direction of the roar. He would strain to see what might be there, and he would wiggle his whiskers hoping to sense something in the air. What could it be, he wondered?

Jeremy scurried up to a fellow mouse and asked him, "Brother Mouse, do you hear a sound, a roaring in your ears?"

The other mouse didn't even bother to lift his whiskers out of the ground. He was too busy. "No, no, I don't hear anything. And besides, I don't have time to talk." And off he went before Jeremy had a chance to say anything more.

Not to be easily discouraged, Jeremy decided to ask another mouse the same question. Maybe this mouse had heard the sound.

The second mouse looked at him in a most peculiar way. "Sound? What sound?" And before Jeremy could stop him long enough to describe what he had heard, the second mouse scampered off, disappearing behind the pines.

When none of the other mice knew anything about the sound, Jeremy decided that the best thing he could do would be to forget about the whole thing and get busy. He knew how to be a busy little mouse. And so he started hurrying and scurrying to and fro once more.

But no matter how busy he was, he would still hear the sound. He tried to pretend that it had disappeared. But even when he tried not to hear it, he knew it was still there!

Jeremy became more and more curious about the sound. So one day, he decided to go off by himself and investigate. It was easy to scurry off from the other mice. They were too busy to notice he had gone, anyway.

When he was off by himself, the sound was stronger and much clearer. Now he could sit quietly and listen hard.

Jeremy stood on the edge of Mouse Village and looked back at the only life he had ever known. He sat listening to the sound for a long time. But he knew he could no longer be content to just listen. It was time to discover more about this sound. He turned to face another direction. He looked out into the darkness of the vast unknown and boldly left Mouse Village.

Jeremy was listening hard to the sound in the distance, when suddenly he heard someone say, "Hello, Little Brother." Jeremy was so startled he almost ran away. "Hello," again said the voice. It sounded friendly enough.

"Who are you?" asked the timid little mouse.

"It is I, Brother Raccoon. You are all by yourself, Little Brother," said the raccoon. "What are you doing here all alone?"

Jeremy was embarrassed. He didn't want to have to talk to anybody about the sound. Especially not after what happened in Mouse Village.

"I heard a sound," he said timidly. "A roaring in my ears and I am investigating it."

"A roaring in your ears? You mean the River," said the raccoon, without any hesitation. "Come, walk with me. I will take you there."

"Once I find out about this River, I can go back to my work and my life in Mouse Village," thought Jeremy. "Why, I will even ask Raccoon to return with me. If the mice in the village don't believe me, they will surely believe a raccoon."

Little Mouse walked close behind the raccoon, so as to be sure not to lose his way. His heart was pounding. He had never known such excitement. They wound their way through a cathedral forest of tall evergreens. There was an intoxicating smell of pine and cedar. As they drew closer to the River, the sound became louder. The air became cooler, and there was a fine mist. There was a sense that something important was about to happen. Suddenly, they came to the River! The mighty River! It was so huge that Little Mouse could not see across it. And it roared, loudly, rushing swiftly on its course, coming from some other place, going to the great unknown.

"It's powerful!" the little mouse said, fumbling for words.

"Yes, the river is a great thing," answered Raccoon, "but here, let me introduce you to a friend."

In a smoother, shallower place was a lily pad,

bright and green. Sitting upon it was a frog, almost as green as the pad it sat on. The frog's white belly stood out clearly.

"Hello, Little Brother," said the frog. "Welcome to the river."

"I must leave you now," cut in Raccoon, "but do not fear, Little Brother, for Frog will care for you now."

"Who are you?" Jeremy asked.

"Why, I am a frog."

"A frog?" questioned Jeremy. He had never seen a frog before. "How is it possible to be so far out in the mighty river?"

"That is very easy," said the little frog. "I can go both on land and on water. And I can live both above the water and below in the water. I am the Keeper of the Water."

Jeremy was astonished! He tried to think of words. He had never met the Keeper of the Water. But no words came.

Without hesitating, the frog said, "Little Mouse, would you like some Medicine Power?"

"Medicine Power? Do you mean for me? Yes, of course. What do I do?" asked the eager little mouse.

"It is not that hard. All you need to do is crouch down real low and jump up as high as you can."

"That's all?" asked Jeremy.

"Yes. Crouch down as low as you can and jump up as high as you can! That will give you your medicine!"

Little Mouse did exactly what the frog told him to do. He crouched down as low as he could and jumped as high as he could. And when he did, his eyes saw something even more powerful than the mighty River. He saw the Sacred Mountain.

How long Jeremy gazed at the Sacred Mountain, we can't be sure. For such moments exist in a space somewhere beyond time. But suddenly, everything changed. Instead of landing on familiar ground, the little mouse splashed down in water. And mice, as you know, can't swim very well. Jeremy was terrified. He flailed his legs about, trying to keep head above water, choking and sputtering, struggling for his very life. He was frightened nearly to death. Finally, he managed to make his way to the river bank.

"You tricked me. . .you tricked me!" Little Mouse yelled at the frog.

Undisturbed by Jeremy's screaming, the frog said calmly, "Wait. No harm came to you. You saw the Sacred Mountain, didn't you? Let go of your anger and fear. It can blind you. What matters is what happened. What did you see?"

The little mouse, still shivering from the fear or landing in the water, could hardly speak. He stammered, "The. . .the Sacred Mountain!"

"You are no longer just a little mouse. You have a new name. You are Jumping Mouse."

"Oh, thank you," said a startled Jumping Mouse. "Thank you, thank you."

Jumping Mouse stood up and shook off the water. And he shook off the anger and fear. He thought instead about the beauty of the Sacred Mountain.

He thought, "I must go back and tell my people what has happened." He couldn't wait to share. Surely, they would be eager to hear his stories of the river and the mountain.

With great excitement, Jumping Mouse set off for Mouse Village. Everyone would be so pleased to see him. Why, there might even be a celebration in his honor!

When Jumping Mouse arrived, he was still wet. But it hadn't rained in Mouse Village and everyone else was dry! There was great discussion as to why Jumping Mouse was wet. Could it be that he had been swallowed by some horrible beast and then spit out again? That would mean there was something horribly wrong with this mouse. Fear took hold; who knew what could happen once you left Mouse Village? No one wanted to spend time with Jumping Mouse. His stories about the River and the Sacred Mountain fell on deaf ears.

Even though no one in Mouse Village believed Jumping Mouse, in time it didn't matter. He never forgot his vision of the Sacred Mountain. Jumping Mouse stayed in Mouse Village, but of course now life was different. But then, he was different.

Jumping Mouse settled quietly into life in Mouse Village. For a while, that is. But there came a day when he knew he must leave. The memory of the Sacred Mountain was not one he could forget. He knew that somehow he must find his way there.

Once again, Jumping Mouse went to the edge of Mouse Village and looked out onto the prairie. This time, there was no raccoon waiting. There was no path, even. He knew that now he must find his own way. He looked up in the sky for eagles. It was full of many brown spots, each one an eagle. At any moment, they could swoop down from the sky. Even though his heart was pounding with fear, Jumping Mouse was determined to go to the Sacred Mountain. And so, gathering all his courage, he ran just as fast as he could onto the prairie.

Jumping Mouse ran until he came to a mound of sage. He was safe now, out of view of those brown spots in the sky. He was resting and trying to catch his breath when he saw a kind old mouse, a country gentleman. This patch of sage, which was home for the old mouse, was a haven indeed. There were plentiful seeds, varieties which he had never seen, and material for making nests. So many things for a mouse to be busy with.

"Hello," said the kindly old mouse. "Welcome to my home."

Jumping Mouse was amazed. He had never seen such a place. Or such a mouse! "What a wonderful place you have. You have everything here. And you are even safe from the eagles. I have never seen such a place like this before."

"Yes," smiled the kindly old mouse, "it is safe here. And from here, you can see all the beings of the prairie. Why, there are buffalo and rabbit and coyote and fox and. . ."

Jumping Mouse listened in amazement as the old mouse named every animal of the prairie. Why, he knew all their names by heart!

"Sir, what about the river and the mountains? Can you also see them?"

"Well, little friend, you can certainly see the river. I know of the river. But as to the mountain, I am afraid that does not exist. It is just a myth, a story that people enjoy telling. Young man, take my advice and forget about the mountain. Everything you could want is here. You can stay with me for as long as you like. And besides, this is the best place to be."

For a moment, Jumping Mouse questioned his decision to go to the Sacred Mountain. He was tempted to stay put and make a life here with Country Mouse. It was such a comfortable place. And certainly it was far greater than the life he had known in Mouse Village.

Jumping Mouse listened carefully to the words of Country Mouse, especially what he had to say about the Sacred Mountain.

"How can you say that the Great Mountain is only a myth?" challenged Jumping Mouse. "Once I saw the Sacred Mountain, and it is not something one can ever forget."

Jumping Mouse had his own answer. He knew he must go. He thanked Country Mouse for making him feel so welcome and for sharing his home. "I cannot stay longer. I must go now, to seek the Mountain."

"You are a foolish mouse, indeed, if you leave here. The prairie is a dangerous place, especially for a little mouse! Why, just look up in the sky. The old mouse pointed dramatically to the sky. See up there? Those spots are eagles, just waiting for a little mouse. They can see for miles. And they will catch you!"

Even though Jumping Mouse listened as Country Mouse gave his fearful warnings, and even though in the sky there were still those brown spots. . .Jumping Mouse knew he must make his way to the Sacred Mountain. He stood still for a moment, took a deep breath, gathered his strength, and once again ran with all his might across the prairie.

It was hard for Jumping Mouse to leave the comfortable life with Country Mouse. Out on the prairie was much to be afraid of. As Jumping Mouse gathered all his courage and ran as hard as he could, he could feel the brown spots flying high overhead. Would those brown spots really swoop down and catch him, just as Country Mouse had said? He shivered at the thought. He was truly in the unknown now.

All of a sudden, he ran into a stand of chokecherries. It was a wonderful place to explore. Why, there were things to gather, delicious seeds to eat, and many grasses for making nests. Jumping Mouse was busy investigating his new terrain when he saw an enormous, dark, furry thing lying motionless in the grass. He decided to climb up on it. There was a large mound to explore. There were even horns to climb on. That would be fun, thought Jumping Mouse.

Immediately, he made his way on one of the horns, when all of a sudden he heard a sound. It sounded like a moan. It seemed to come from the dark furry thing! Quick as a wink, Jumping Mouse scurried down to the grass beneath. There was another moan, and the sound of deep breathing.

A voice said, "Hello, my brother."

"Who are you?" asked a curious Jumping Mouse.

"Why I am Buffalo!"

"A buffalo!" thought Jumping Mouse. Even in Mouse Village he had heard of the mighty buffalo!

Jumping Mouse had never before seen a buffalo. Certainly, no buffalo had ever lived in Mouse Village.

"What a magnificent being you are," Jumping Mouse said to Buffalo.

"Thank you, my little brother, for visiting me."

"You are lying down. What is wrong?" asked the little mouse."

"I am sick and I am dying," said Buffalo. "There is only one thing that can save me. That is the eye of a mouse. But there is no such thing as a mouse out here on the prairie!"

The eye of a mouse! Jumping Mouse was astonished! "You mean my tiny little eye could save this magnificent being?" He darted back to the chokecherries. He scurried back and forth. What to do, what to do. But he could hear the breathing of the buffalo. It was slowing down and becoming heavy.

"He will die," thought Jumping Mouse, "if I do not give him my eye. He is such a magnificent being. I cannot let him die."

With no time to waste, Jumping Mouse scurried back to the spot where Buffalo lay. "I am a mouse," he said with a shaky voice. "And you are such a magnificent being. I cannot let you die. I have two eyes. If my eye can save you, I will gladly give it to you."

The minute he spoke, Jumping Mouse's eye flew out of his head and Buffalo was made whole. The buffalo jumped to his feet, shaking Jumping Mouse's whole world.

Buffalo said to Jumping Mouse, "I know that you have been to the River. And I know of your quest to the Sacred Mountain. You have healed me. Because you have given so freely, I will be your brother forever. To cross the prairie, you must run under my belly. I will take you right to the foot of the Sacred Mountain. Have no fear for the spots in the sky. The eagles cannot see you while you run under me, for you will be safely hidden. All they will see is my back. I know the ways of the prairie. You are safe with me."

Even with the confident words from Buffalo, it was frightening to be walking under a buffalo on an wide-open prairie. What about the brown spots? They were still in the sky. And the hooves were scary. What would happen if one landed on a little mouse? With only one eye, it was hard to see well enough to stay out of the way. Each time the buffalo took a step, it felt like the whole world shook. It seemed to take ever so long to walk across the prairie. But finally they stopped.

"This is as far as I go," said Buffalo. "I am a being of the prairie. If I were to take you further, I would fall on you."

"Thank you very much," said Jumping Mouse. "It was frightening crossing the prairie with only one eye. I was so afraid that one of your powerful hooves would land on me!"

"You did not know, my little brother, that there was never any need for fear. For I am a Sundancer, and I am always sure where my hooves land. My time with you is over. I must go back to the prairie. You can always find me there."

With that, Buffalo turned and left.

Jumping Mouse was happy in his new surroundings. There were new things to investigate. There were plants in abundance and new seeds to enjoy. As he was busy exploring this new place, suddenly before him was a gray wolf. The wolf didn't seem to see the little mouse. In fact, he didn't seem to be seeing much of anything. He was just sitting there, doing nothing.

Jumping Mouse was pleased to find a new friend in the woods and spoke to him right away. "Hello, Brother Wolf."

Immediately, the wolf's ears sat up and he became alert. He looked directly at Jumping Mouse. "Am I a wolf? Yes, that is what I am. Wolf! Wolf! I am a wolf!" He seemed quite pleased with his new discovery. But then his mind dimmed again, and in a matter of minutes he had forgotten completely who he was!

Several times the same sequence occurred. The wolf would just sit, quietly staring out into nothingness, completely without memory as to who he was. Jumping Mouse would say, "But you are a mighty being. You are a wolf."

"Yes," would come the answer from the gray wolf. "I am a wolf! Yes, now I remember. That is what I am!" He would become excited once again, but soon would forget again.

"Such a great being," thought Jumping Mouse, "but he has no memory. He has forgotten who he is."

Jumping Mouse would help the wolf remember who he was for a moment, but then he would forget again. Jumping mouse wanted to help his new friend. "If giving up an eye could help the buffalo, then maybe I could give up my eye to the wolf and he would be well, too." This time there was no hurrying and scurrying around. And there was no need to ask anyone else for advice. He knew how to find his own answer. This time, he went to a peaceful spot and sat quietly. In the silence, he listened to his heart. It told him exactly what he must do.

Wasting no time, Jumping Mouse hurried back to where the wolf was.

"Brother Wolf," he called out.

"Wolf? Wolf?" came the still-confused response.

"Brother Wolf, listen to me. I know now what will heal you. If I could give an eye to a buffalo and it would heal him, then I will gladly give you my eye."

No sooner had he said the words than the last eye of the little mouse flew out of his head. Now Jumping Mouse had no eyes. But that didn't seem to matter so much. What mattered was that the wolf was whole again. He could remember who he was.

As soon as the eye of the mouse went into the wolf, he was healed.

Tears started to flow down the wolf's face. Of course, Jumping Mouse could not see him because he had no eyes. He was blind. But even without eyes, he could see that the wolf was whole again. Now, the wolf could remember who he was.

"Thank you, Jumping Mouse. You have healed me," said the wolf, as tears ran down his cheeks. "Thank you, my little friend. Now I can remember many things. I am the guide to the Sacred Mountain and to the Great Medicine Lake. And it is your time to go there. You are blind, so you must follow close beside me. But I know the way, and I will take you there."

The wolf, with his little friend close by, slowly made his way through the tall pine trees to the edge of the Sacred Lake. Unlike the river which roared as it rushed over rocks, the lake sat in perfect stillness. "This lake," said the wolf, "is more powerful even than the mighty river. For this is a Medicine Lake. It reflects all the world, all the people of the world, the lodges of the people, and all the beings of the prairies and the skies. It is said that he who drinks of this Sacredness is given the wisdom to understand the mysteries of life."

Jumping Mouse leaned down and drank the cool, refreshing water from the Sacred Lake.

The wolf said, "This is where I must leave you, little friend, for I must return. There are others I must guide. But if you want, I will stay with you for a while."

"Thank you, my brother, but you must go, and it is my time to be alone." Even though Jumping Mouse was trembling with fear, he said goodbye to his friend.

Jumping Mouse stood alone and trembling, sensing what was to come. He knew, somehow, that an eagle would find him. All of a sudden he could feel a shadow on his back. Then he heard the noise of a giant eagle swooping down, coming closer. He braced himself for what was to come. . .the noise grew louder, an enormous swoosh. . .then, a thump on his back. Jumping Mouse fell into a deathlike sleep.

After a while—we have no way of knowing how long, since time in such experiences has no meaning—Jumping Mouse began to awaken. The surprise of being alive was great. And he could see! Even though everything was blurry, he could see colors and they were beautiful.

"I can see! I can see!" said Jumping Mouse again and again.

A blurry shape started to move near Jumping Mouse. Jumping Mouse squinted hard, trying to see, but the shape remained a blur.

"Hello, brother," a familiar voice said. "Do you want some medicine?"

"Some medicine? Me? Yes! Yes!"

"Then," said the voice, "what you must do is crouch down as low as you can, and jump as high as you can."

Jumping Mouse did exactly what he was told. He crouched as low as he could and jumped as high as he could! Suddenly, a wind caught him and began to lift him higher and higher.

"Do not be afraid!" the assuring voice called out. "Ride the wind. Hang on to it. It will carry you. . .TRUST!"

Jumping Mouse did as he was told. He closed his eyes and let go. The wind began to carry him. The wind, the breath of Great Spirit, lifted him higher and higher. This time, when Jumping Mouse opened his eyes, they were clear. The higher he went, the clearer they became. He could see with the eyes of an eagle. He could see through things and into things. He could see miles away. He could see in the Spirit Way.

As Jumping Mouse looked down, way below was his old familiar friend. There was the frog, sitting on a lily pad on the beautiful Medicine Lake.

"You have a new name," called the frog. "You are no longer Jumping Mouse. You are Eagle!"

References

Bolen, Jean Shinoda. *The Tao of Psychology*. San Francisco: Harper & Row, 1982.

Bradshaw, John. *Creating Love: The Next Stage of Growth*. New York: Bantam, 1992.

Campbell, Joseph. *The Hero With a Thousand Faces*. Princeton: Bollingen Series.

Campbell, Joseph. *The Masks of God: Creative Mythology*. New York; Viking, 1968.

Cooper, David A. "Invitation to the Soul." *Parabola, XIX*, no. 1 (February 1994):7-11.

Course in Miracles: Workbook for Students. Huntington Station, New York: Coleman Graphics, 1975.

Dorff, Francis. *The Art of Passingover*. New York: Integration Books, 1988.

Eliot, T.S. *Four Quartets*. Byrnt Norton, New York: Harcourt Brace Jovanovich, 1943.

Eliot, T.S. *The Love Song of J. Alfred Prufrock*. In *Modern American & Modern British Poetry* by Louis Untermeyer. New York: Harcourt, Brace and Company.

Hesse, Herman. *Siddhartha*. Translated by Hilda Rosner. New York: New Directions Publishing Company, 1951.

The I Ching. The Richard Wilhelm translation rendered into English by Cary F. Baynes. Bollingen Series XIX, Princeton University Press, 1950.

Jongeward, David. *Weaver of Worlds*. Rochester, Vermont: Destiny Books, 1990.

Lionel, Frederic. *Challenge: On Special Mission*. Great Britain: Biddles, Ltd., Guildford and King's Lynn, 1980.

Markides, Kyriacos C. *Homage to the Sun*. London: Arkana, 1987.

Nichols, Sallie. *Jung and Tarot: An Archetypal Journey*. York Beach, Maine: Samuel Weiser, Inc., 1980.

Storm, Hyemeyohsts. *Seven Arrows*. New York: Ballentine Books, 1972.

Sugrue, Thomas. *There is a River*. New York: Henry Holt & Company, 1942.

About the Author

Mary Elizabeth Marlow is a transpersonal teacher, author, intuitive counselor, international speaker, and seminar leader. She is the author of *Handbook for the Emerging Woman* and co-author, with Joseph Rael, of *Being and Vibration.* She has spoken to a wide variety of audiences and has been featured in a number of international magazines, including *New Woman, Livs Lyst, Human Potential, Libelle, Onkruid, Human Potential Resources, Hjemmet,* and *Libelle.*

Mary Elizabeth draws from a rich and eclectic background which provides the basis for both her writing and her teaching. Her academic background includes a degree in English with a minor in religion and fine arts, graduate work in counseling, and certification with Dr. Carl and Stephanie Simonton as a cancer therapist.

Her primary education, however, has been from life itself. What was once a childhood interest in exploring the unifying Spirit behind all traditions deepened to become a lifetime quest. Her many journeys, which have included visits to Europe, India, Egypt, and the Middle East, have allowed her to interface with the mysteries and metaphors of a variety of traditions and cultures.

Recognized as a gifted story-teller and ritualist, Mary Elizabeth brings a unique approach to the transformational process. She has the ability to absorb the inner meanings of the great ancient stories and to juxtapose them with experiences from her own life and with stories of those she has encountered along the way.

She invites her readers to pause and sense their own inner alliance with the collective wisdom of the great stories, to be inspired through the experiences of others on the path, and to awaken to their own truth.

Mary Elizabeth serves a guide to many in the seminars and retreats she conducts world-wide. In Europe, she teaches in Greece, Norway, Holland, and England. In the United States, she offers programs in Virginia Beach, Virginia, where she lives, and gives seminars and lectures in a number of other locations.

Noted for her innovative and creative approaches to inner healing, Mary Elizabeth has developed a number of original in-depth processes which she uses with individuals, with groups, and in one-day family sessions. She is uniquely gifted in being able to identify and facilitate the healing of core patterns and issues and to empower others with a new sense of their authentic selves.

For information on Schedules, Books, or Tapes, contact:
Mary Elizabeth Marlow, 903 Goldsboro Avenue
Virginia Beach, VA 23451 * (804) 425-7452